Dead Asleep

by

Jenna Slone

authorHOUSE™

1663 LIBERTY DRIVE, SUITE 200
BLOOMINGTON, INDIANA 47403
(800) 839-8640
WWW.AUTHORHOUSE.COM

First published by AuthorHouse 09/29/05

ISBN: 1-4208-7580-9 (sc)

Printed in the United States of America
Bloomington, Indiana

This book is printed on acid-free paper.

TABLE OF CONTENTS

This book is dedicated to : My Mom. This would not have been possible, without her. My Daughters. THEY are my inspiration. My Father, who has always supported me.

Special Thanks to : Kathy for supplying me with needed writing material. Pat for keeping me in ink, and much needed moral support.

Melinda for being the Dear Friend that she is

My fellow compatriots, at Five County Drug and Alcohol Program, who have helped me find my purpose.

In Memory Of: The man who's life I took.

Daryl—My Dear Friend who left me more than memento's. To always be proud of who and what you are.

<u>Introduction…...</u>

My name is Jenna, and this is a true account of my experiences, to the best of my memory and knowledge.

Not only do I feel it is important to tell other's that no matter how bad things can get, to never give-up hope, that things CAN improve! The most important message I have is this: DO NOT EVER DRINK AND DRIVE!!! Do NOT think it will never happen to you. I did. This wheelchair proves me wrong! It took something so catastrophic to open my eyes, will it take this, to open yours? I obviously have bad luck, sure. But, luck does not change the fact, that this was MY OWN FAULT. If I had been sober, that man would be alive today, and I would not be permanently handicapped. It's as simple, as that. Do not take life for granted! Be grateful for ALL that you have! And, for all whom you love. And, visa versa. I believe that everyone has something to offer. We ALL have a special purpose. Please, don't make it take something like this, to find yours.

I have finally found contentment in living my life, the best way that I can. Appreciative of things I used to take for granted, SOBER, more Spiritual, happy, grateful for all I have, and a better person, in general. Pass my message on. Tell them to read this book! I really care about other's, I would not wish this on my worst enemy. Not even on husbands! Have a good life.

A FRIEND,

Jenna Slone

CHEMISTRY 101

Here she was, sitting on a bar stool again, looking for a way out of this awful marriage. Tonight was Taco Night at the local tavern, and she was enjoying hers with a beer, as usual. Jenna started a conversation with the bar-waitress there, not being a shy person. They started talking about generalities at first, and that led to talk of bad relationships they had had. She had taken her wedding rings off before she went to the bar, not wanting to admit that she was, indeed married. Jenna kept her eyes peeled for eligible men. She had always got along better with men than she did women. Jenna had always been a passionate, sexual person. She loved her husband, she just didn't like him very much ! So, here she was, looking for answers in the wrong place.

Jenna had been married to her second husband seven years. Seven tumultuous years ! They had five children between them, and were both in their second marriages. Don had three children and Jenna had one, from previous marriages. They also had a daughter , together. She had been born premature and had a serious heart condition. It was a high maintenance family, to say the least ! His kids called her Mom and she did her best to be so. Jenna also kept a full-time job, as their bills were so high. She did her best to keep their four bedroom house clean and also did a lot of the yard work. She spent most of her spare time in the flower beds. She should have been happy with all that she had, but she wasn't. Yes, her husband could be verbally, and physically abusive, but it was her own insecurity that led her astray.

As the waitress and Jenna talked, the question of if she was married came up. Jenna told her no, that she was newly divorced and looking to meet someone. They had introduced their selves earlier, she said her name was Jennifer. Jennifer said she had a single cousin, who was there tonight, and she was sure that he would like to meet her also. Jenna said, "Bring it on, baby !"She laughed as she turned and walked away. Jenna quickly checked her make-up, ran her fingers through her hair, and secretly hoped he wasn't a dog. Jennifer was only gone a few minutes when a very, tall man with a short, pony tail walked up to me. They introduced themselves, shook hands and made small talk. When he smiled, she noticed that one of his front teeth was going bad, but he seemed really nice. She also noticed him looking at her ring finger, so she told him that she had just got divorced. It was summer time, and her wedding rings had left a tell-tale mark from her tan. He invited her to sit at his table, so she did. His name was Steve, and he introduced me to his friend Billy, and his girlfriend, Margaret. Jenna joined Steve in a game of pool. It was obvious from the start, that they shared the same quirky sense of humor! They laughed a lot that night and she was very glad to have met him. Later, sitting at the table alone, (Billy had left to take Margaret home), they had a nice chat. All of a sudden, she leaned over the table and kissed him ! She just wanted to !Ever since they had shook hands, the chemistry was there. It was very strong. Jenna knew that they both felt it, too.

Jenna asked Steve if she had been too forward, when she kissed him. He said, "No, he had enjoyed it !" He kissed her again, and asked her if she wanted to go to the next town's bar. (That was Steve's home town.) She said, "Sure !She would love to go." Jenna excused herself, and made a quick stop in the Little Girl's Room. She did her business, then checked out her appearance in the full-length mirror. Jenna had lost a few pounds, and was glad about that, now !! She was wearing her tight, white jeans, a sleeveless vest, and her velvet sandles. She shook her head to let her hair fall in place, in a sexy way, licked her lips and whet her lip gloss, and last but not least, sprayed a little perfume . Steve was waiting outside the restroom door. He proceeded to tell her how some girls wore so much more make-up when they came out, than when they went in, it was hard to recognize them ! That was only one of the times that night that Jenna about split a gut, laughing so hard ! Jenna liked this guy. So far. She was not very astute, when it came to men ! Just then, Billy walked in and asked for a ride home. His car had broken down on the way back from Margaret's. Steve asked if she minded, that it was on the way. Jenna said that she didn't mind.

So, the three of them took off for Billy's Mobile Home. All the way to his house, he complained about Margaret. How he was tired of one woman being in his life; his bed. On and on he went. Jenna was thinking to herself, "What a male- chauvenist-pig !" She kept quiet for as long as she could. Her tongue hurt from biting it ! She finally couldn't take it any more ! "Why are you with her then?" "Why do keep screwing her, because it's convenient ?!" Steve laughed. "I think you've finally met your match Billy!" He had made Jenna livid! She was so glad when they dropped him off. Plus, she wanted time alone with Steve. They went on to the bar. They had another beer, listened to the DJ, and talked some more. They discovered they had a lot in common. They both loved to read, liked many of the same movies, and both had life-long friends. He asked for her phone number, but she knew she couldn't give him her home phone number! Jenna gave him her work, phone number. She was there most of the time anyhow ! Many kisses later, he took her back to her car. Jenna went home with a big smile on her face that night !

When Jenna got home, she made love to her husband. Yes, love. A part of her still loved him. Part of her life with him was so good. The other part was so bad. Jenna really wanted a solid marriage, one like her parents had. She wanted a twenty-fifth, a fiftieth, all of that ! But, after all that had happened, she couldn't get over the part of her that hated him. Jenna just loved sex ! Always had. She knows now, that was the part of her that was forever looking for acceptance, affection. Having never known her "true" family background or heritage; who she looked like, or was related to; had a negative influence on her self-esteem. Having sex with men; known or unknown; helped re-enforce her confidence. Temporarily. All of the shrinks she had went to; those so-called professionals; not one of them had ever been able to tell her, or her adopted parents, what was wrong with her, why she felt this way. Maybe, most patients didn't have a frigging Harvard degree, but who knew their bodies better than they did ? They lived in them, didn't they ?!

Next morning, Jenna went to work. Six to two, at a nearby Nursing Home. She worked mainly in the laundry, but on some days ran the electric floor machines and did other house keeping duties. Jenna had always enjoyed doing laundry. How she wished life was that simple ! Put it in dirty, stained, smelly, and pull it out clean, fresh, and like new. Nothing to do with reality was that easy !

Jenna was in a good mood all of that day. She walked around with a silly grin on her face, even humming out loud ! She told one girl that she worked with, about meeting Steve. Ok. Bragged. It felt good to be wanted. Jenna's name was announced on the loud speaker, asking her to come to the main Nurse's station. A warm feeling stole over her body. Steve was on the phone! Just hearing his voice got her panties wet ! He had written her phone number on a small piece of pink paper, and kept it in his wallet. Steve showed it to Jenna years later. It's probably been used as a spit-ball by now !

LIVING A LIE

This started the part dream, part nightmare of seeing him, whenever she could, and lying her way out of it. When Jenna was with him, life was good. He knew about her daughter's, they were a part of her; no matter what. Of course, Jenna had told him she was single, divorced twice. Jenna told him that she married her first husband at eighteen. Toooo damned young!! But, hey,Jenna knew it ALL!! Doesn't every teenager? The marriage only lasted three years, but they loved each other deeply. They created a beautiful daughter from this short, but intense union. Looked like him, acted like her. And then she was re-married at twenty-seven, to her second and current husband, Don. Steve told her later, that he thought she was still married, as the tan marks on her ring finger, gave her away! Jenna had a thin, gold wedding band, and a small coribichon emerald engagement ring. Nothing grand, but she had never needed anything grand. Jenna loved them because they had been given to her in love. At the time, she wore a size four ring! Nice and thin! In pretty good shape too! Working a lot and running after kids helped. Jenna had just added "cook" to her job description at the Nursing Home. She had always loved to cook. She had attended a Vocational High School, her junior and senior years, and took a cooking course. Jenna quit, November of her senior year, with an A&B average grade, to marry her first husband. She wasn't even knocked-up! Of course, everyone suspected she was. Jenna was just horny, and stupid.

Jenna needed to work as many hours, as the Nursing Home would give her, as she wanted to move out so badly! She had decided that she wasn't taking his crap, any more! After the incident with Jasmine, and what his own son had done to his own daughter, how could she continue to live with this man?

Jasmine was her niece/daughter. Jenna's sister, Fawn, had been incarcerated on a drug charge, and had Jasmine in prison. Their Mom, who was so sick with her Diabetes, talked Fawn out of giving her up for adoption. Her and my Father went to the prison hospital and picked Jasmine up, and brought her home. They kept her for the first weekend, then Jenna insisted that she come stay with her. She knew that she was too much for her Mom! So, even though Jenna already had five kids, and a full-time job, she loved and respected her Mom enough to agree, Jasmine should stay with the family. Don was out of work right then, and said he would help with the baby. And he did. He changed her, bathed her, dressed her, gave her bottles and breathing treatments, and held and kissed her. Which wasn't hard to do, as she was so adorable and kissable!! Jasmine had a sweet disposition, and hardly ever fussed. The older children were great with her, and she would light up, when she heard them. Jasmine's favorite snack was graham crackers. Every time she fussed, the kids ran for the box!

Jasmine stayed with our family from the time she was four days old, until she was fourteen months old. She was a joy to have, and Jenna misses her, more than she can express. Jenna was a busy girl, at this time, but she still managed to make it to the bar often. She never went for the booze. Jenna's close friend bartended there, and like the song from Cheers says, "Where everybody knows your name...". She often said , she went there to talk to people over the age of ten! Sure, it was nice to hear occasional compliments! All Don ever cared about, was a clean house, a baby-sitter, and grub on the table! Oh, and if you happened to mow the grass for him too, that was a bonus. Don's mother was one of those mother-in-laws, that give them all a bad name. Nothing was good enough for her baby boy!! She even denied her own Grand-Daughter, Charlise, right in front of her once, and to this day, Charlise will not identify her as her grandmother, but only use her first name.

Don and Jenna were attempting to adopt Jasmine. They looked at it as just a technicality anyhow! She was already theirs, as far as they were concerned. She was a gorgeous, little, doll! She had dark, curly hair, and big, dark eyes, with long, curling eyelashes. Jasmine was mulatto, which did not mean anything to Jenna! She could have been purple, for all she cared !! Most of Jenna's, and Don's family were prejudiced, and Jasmine "cured" many of them, of that attitude. Or, so she thought.

Fawn finally got released from prison. She sweet-talked Mom into taking Jasmine for the weekend. Jenna thought Jasmine was staying at their house for the weekend. Mom knew Jenna didn't trust Fawn, and Don liked her even less! Fawn was living with her low-life boyfriend, in the bad part of town. He thought he was so bad, in his leather jacket, flinging his long hair back, trying to be a heavy-metal rock star's replica!!

They had Jasmine for less than twenty-four hours, when they took her to the local Child Welfare office, to give her back!! They couldn't handle her! Fawn could do that without notifying Jenna and Don, as she was the biological mother. Jenna says, "Big deal." You have to have a license to drive a car, or a permit to build-on to your house, but anyone can have a child! And, give it away. When Fawn or Jasmine never showed back up at Jenna's Mom's, Estelle got worried and called Jenna. When Estelle told her what had happened, Jenna went ballistic!! Don just got out of Jenna's way. He knew how pissed, and worried she was.

Jenna had a rough, and tough girlfriend that lived not far from Fawn's apartment. She picked her up on the way, and Jenna told her what was going on. Fawn lived on the second story. Jenna's friend stood around the corner from Fawn's door. Jenna kept pounding on the door, yelling for Fawn. Her boyfriend finally answered. Jenna grabbed him by the front of his shirt, and demanded, "Where's Jasmine?" He didn't answer as fast as she would have liked, so she proceeded to beat the snot out of him! All the while yelling for her sister through the closed door. Chicken Shit. Jenna's friend kept sticking her head around the corner, to see if she was ok, or needed any help. After she'd get done laughing, she'd say, "Guess not!"

Fawn's dipshit finally admitted, that they had dumped her at CSB. One of the times Jenna ever heard Don laugh so hard, was when Fawn's boyfriend called the house to tell on Jenna, for beating him up!!

Jenna continued to see Steve whenever she could get away. Things were getting more and more passionate. They hadn't done "The Deed" yet, but they both knew it wouldn't be long! Jenna had Jasmine on her mind, and wasn't too concerned with much else. Don and Jenna finally made arrangements to visit Jasmine, at CSB, once a week. After having her live in their home, for all those months, with no questions asked, they now had to have Supervised visits!! Jenna believes that was the beginning of the end, of this whole situation. As far as Don was concerned. Between this and the affair, the stress was weighing heavily on her heart. They went to see Jasmine every Thursday, so she went to see her relatives in Michigan that Friday, and stayed the weekend. Jenna needed some time away from all this. Her, and her Aunt went garage saleing, in the rich people's neighborhood, and Jenna found some real deals! It always made her feel better, when she bought the kid's stuff. Jenna hadn't called Steve before she left, and was trying to decide if she should end this thing, or not. Jenna was starting to have real feelings for him. She had not planned on this.

DECISIONS..........
DECISIONS

The weekend with her relatives in Michigan had been refreshing, and Jenna thought she had set her mind on ending the affair. She told the nurse's at work that if Steve called, to tell him that she couldn't come to the phone. Jenna knew that if she heard his voice, she would cave! In the meantime, her and Don were arguing all the time. With all the work, between work and home, Jenna's ego needed stroked. Six kids, two in diapers, two growing boys, and both little ones with serious health problems. Jasmine finally got to come home full-time, and Jenna was a busy girl! Jazzy had asthma, and needed breathing treatments, at least once a day. Charlise had a serious heart condition, and needed constant consideration. She hadn't been born with it, but had developed it around age three. She had been born with a low birth rate; three and a half pounds. Jenna's OB/GYN had figured she was only about two weeks early. Jenna's Doctor was a kind, jolly, Italian, who said the baby had Fetal Growth Retardation. Jenna was guilty of smoking during her pregnancy, and knew Charlise's low birth weight was her own fault. Jenna had had a repeat C-Section, as she had so many problems giving birth to Nichole. Charlise was slow at walking, teeth coming in, and speech. She had really cute nicknames for her brother's and sister's, as she could not say their given names, yet. She could be hard to understand, if you weren't around her very much. Charlise was very close to her Grandparents, whom she called, "Mimi and Papa." These were Jenna's adopted parents. Real to her!

Jenna's Mom babysat for her when she had to work, sick as she was with her Diabetes, and all the complications associated with it. That was another great source of stress for Jenna, as she was very close to her Mom, and felt guilty about her babysitting. Jenna felt like she could tell her Mom anything, and she knew all about Steve. Estelle knew how bad things had gotten with Don, and just wanted her Jenna to be happy. Jenna's Mom was going to meet Steve this Saturday. Jenna was going to have Steve pick her up here, for their "birthday" date. She had felt badly about ignoring him, and had finally called him. Jenna needed the attention.

For Jenna's birthday, Steve was taking her out to a nice dinner, and then to see George Carlin, at the Theatre House. They both loved Carlin! Steve told Jenna there was a surprise afterwards, so she guessed he was taking her to a Motel. You could light a cigarette off their combined heat! Jenna had a credit card, at the time, and made good use of it. She went to Victoria's Secret, and bought some lingerie, black, silk stockings, and a garter belt. Jenna knew that black was Steve's favorite color, so she wore a skin-tight, black dress, and some of what she had purchased earlier. Jenna looked HOT!! She felt even hotter! The whole night was fabulous. They laughed their asses off at Carlin, and made mad, passionate love, at the "surprise." Jenna hadn't felt so fulfilled in a very, long time. Now, if only her girl's liked him! That was the "real" test.

Jenna had always felt like a caregiver. She had raised Don's and other's kids, and almost always had the neighborhood in her yard! She actually preferred it that way. That way, she knew where her own were! Don's three kids were by his first wife, Corrie. Jenna called her, Whorrie. Jenna realized that she had short comings of her own, but Corrie was something else! She would sleep with ANYONE. (And, probably had!) She had eventually married her first cousin! Jenna thinks she ran out of strangers. Corrie was a lousy mother. She always put men WAY before her own children! Sex was the most important thing in her life.

Don was to be paid a WHOPPING $ 16.00 a week, for three kids. That's Child Support? How do you support them on that? That didn't even cover their lunch money!! And, she was thousands of dollars in arrearage for not even paying that. How pitiful is that. The real shame, (one of them) was that she hardly ever used her visitation periods. The children missed her, needed their mom, but she had more important things to do. Like cousins.

Jenna never asked, or made Don's kids call her Mom. They asked her, if it would be all right if they did. How could she say no? Jenna grew to love them, and treat them as they were hers, quickly. That, was the easy part. She had fallen "in love" with them, easier than she had their own Father! Corrie was a constant thorn in the side of their marriage. Don was often too defensive of her, as she was the biological mother. Jenna, on the other hand, wanted to protect the children. She saw how badly their mother had hurt them, and just wanted Corrie to stop playing her juvenile games. How many times had Jenna watched the kid's look of disappointment, when she didn't show up for visitation, yet again?

Jenna's parents immediately treated them as their Grandchildren. They may have favored their "real" Grandkids, but they NEVER showed it. Every Holiday, birthday, special occasion, they were not forgotten. And, Grandma and Grandpa went to almost all of anything they had going on at school. Don's kids seemed to blossom with all of their love and attention! The older children treated Charlise and Jasmine as "real" sisters, also. Don and Jenna's house was never a boring place.

Jenna also tried to help at her Mom's whenever she could. When her Mom had open-heart surgery, Jenna kept her at her house, while she recovered. She fixed up the boy's bedroom for her, and moved them to the fold-out couch. Jenna put a hospital bed in the room, to make it easier for her to get in and out of bed. She had a girl-friend come and help scrub down the house for germs, and tried to cook, heart-healthy meals. The children all loved having Grandma stay! Jenna did too. Estelle would still read to the kids, and was always ready for a hug. As a surprises to Mom, while she recovered, Jenna's Dad re-modeled their bathroom, and Jenna fixed up her bedroom.

She painted it, scrubbed the carpet, and bought new curtains and bedspread. The bedspread was too big, so Estelle made a matching valance with the extra material. She was so talented, that way! It turned out nice, and Mom was thrilled!

After her birthday, Jenna went around with a silly grin on her face. Everything her and Steve did together, made her so happy! She was just waiting for the right time to leave Don. Jenna had left him before, but always came back, for the kid's sake. This time, it would be the FINAL time. One of Jenna's bosses names was Steve, so talking on the phone was easy. "Mom, it's work calling!" She felt little guilt at the time, as Don was almost always drunk, and sometimes abusive. Jenna appreciated all of the things Don had provided. But, she earned a lot of it too, and had to put up with his ex-slut , to boot!! Don did not know how to love a person, completely. He had never experienced it, so how could he give it?

THE STRAW THAT BROKE THE CAMEL'S BACK

That's where Jenna was today, in the flowerbeds. She loved to have her hands in the dirt, watching things she had planted, spring into life; grow. Jenna had flowerbeds all around her house, with a rock garden out back, several blooming Yucca's, Rose bushes, Lilies, Laitris, Flowering Cactus, and Morning Glories on her fence. Jenna knew a guy in the Landscape Business, and had recently purchased two new trees, that he planted next to her new driveway, that led to Don's new baby, the pole-barn. They were a Crab-Apple and a Dogwood. They would both bloom in time, also. Jenna had brought some starts from her Mother's yard, and was babying them into growth. A Lilac Bush, a Honeysuckle plant, and the Snowball bush was already going great guns! Jenna loved anything that flowered, but also had different plants, mostly perennials, that added green to the landscape. Jenna took great pride in her gardens. She had received many comments and compliments. This all took little money, just hard work, patience, and diligence. Jenna had to break, get cleaned-up and take CJ school shopping.

Jenna had recently sold her Cutlass, and was spending the last of the profits on CJ's clothes. She had given the majority to Don's DWI lawyer. If she had all the money she had spent on drugs, and lawyer's, she could buy a brand new car, with CASH. More hindsight. After all that had had just occurred with CJ and Charlise, she was still going to make sure he had an adequate wardrobe for school. Jenna had already shopped for the other four, with CJ hedging going with her until now. She knew he felt uncomfortable about being alone with her. Jenna wasn't crazy about the idea herself! Once again, she put her responsibilities as a parent, ahead of her own misgivings. Anyone, that said, she didn't still love him, deep down, didn't really know her. She blamed a lot of his problems on his unfit mother. But, Jenna also would accept fault, for her part. CJ had problems later in his life that Jenna attributes to his youthful problems. Jenna had tried to get him into counseling, but Don wouldn't hear of it! "No son of his was going to air his dirty laundry in front of a stranger! It's none of their damned business!!" Don said that if CJ needed to talk to someone, he could talk to him! They never did, as far as she knows.

One day last week, Jenna came home from work to find Charlise in tears. Jenna pulled her aside, and asked her quietly, "What's wrong, Sweetheart?" As she has stated earlier, Charlise had nicknames for the older children, and her name for CJ was CoCo. Charlise took her Mommy's head, and pulled it closer to her mouth. She whispered in her ear, "CoCo owed my pee-pee." She had a look of terror on her little face. Jenna reached right down, and scooped her up into her arms. They stood there a moment, with Jenna held her Baby close, rocking her, telling her, that she would take care of it, it would never happen again! Jenna took Charlise into the bathroom, had Charlise take her bottoms off, and examined her, thoroughly. What she saw, almost made her physically ill. Charlise had definitely been touched, messed with, molested. By then, Charlise was sobbing, as was her Mom! Jenna asked her other questions relating to her molestation, but, Charlise was so upset, she couldn't even be understood by Mom. Jenna took her into the family room, gave her some tissue and a juicebox ,and put her favorite Disney movie into the VCR. Jenna asked if she was hungry, and Charlise shook her head no, vehemently!

CJ had walked out the door, as soon as Jenna walked in, and Jenna was glad he wasn't in the same house with her right now!! Jenna was like a bull in distress. Steam coming from her ears, foam coming from her mouth. If she had confronted him then, she might have hurt him! Jenna began to get things together for supper. She was angrily tossing things around, not really conscious of her actions. Lizzy walked into the kitchen, unaware of what had happened, and merrily asked, "What's for dinner, Mom?" "I'm starving." "Lunch today, was the pits!" Jenna turned towards her and said, "What? What d'you say Liz ?" " I asked what was for dinner. Are you ok, Mom?" Elizabeth was a sweetheart to ask. Jenna did not want to tell her what had happened. She didn't want her to lose faith in the outside world, let alone knowing your own brother had done something to destroy your trust in mankind! Jenna hoped he had never done this to the other girl's! How was she to really know?!

Just as supper was finished, and Jenna was ready to dish up plates, Don came in the door. She would wait 'til supper was over, to tell him. But, how was she to ask Charlise to sit at the same table as CJ? She went into the family room, and squatted down next to her, and told her supper was ready, to come and eat. Charlise asked if Daddy was home. Her Mom told her, that yes he was home, she would tell him what happened after supper. Just then, CJ came in. Don said, "Hey, CJ, school ok?" CJ grunted, shrugged his shoulders, as if to say, "Same as usual." They all sat and had supper. Jenna thought family meals were so important. To have that intimate time spent, talking about the day. Charlise and CJ were quiet. They passed on the desert Jenna was passing out.

After Jenna and Gary had cleared the table, and loaded the dishwasher, she put the pans to soak, and went in to talk to her husband. She asked him if they could go in the bedroom, that she needed to talk to him in private. Jenna proceeded to tell him what happened. He didn't believe it. "What? How do you know?" Jenna said, "Because, Charlise told me! And her privates confirmed it!!" Don put his head down, and shook it violently. "I'll ask him, but I can't believe he would do that." He left to go and confront his son. CJ denied it, and blamed Jenna for making it up. Don left it at that.

Later, that evening her and Don had another, knock-down, drag-out. Jenna wanted to get CJ some help, she even suggested a psychiatrist. Don was adamant about his innocence, "He is fine! You're the one who's crazy, needs help!" Jenna said she wanted to leave him. "And go where? Who's going to take you in, and take your shit, like I do?" Jenna was sobbing loudly. "Shut up, you big baby! If you think you're taking Charlise anywhere, think again. Just leave it alone, Jenna. Or, you'll be sorry." Don turned, and left the room.

Jenna didn't sleep much that night. She unfortunately, knew Don was correct on one count. Where the Hell would she go? She didn't make enough to have her own place, raise two kids, and pay medical bills. She knew she was always welcome at home, but with her Mom so sick, she did not want to be a bigger burden than she already felt. This, is when she started looking for a way out, in earnest! Next morning, before school, she promised Charlise she would never be alone with CJ again. She never was. To Jenna's knowledge.

When Don and Jenna first married, his ex-wife, Corrie, had custody of their daughter, Elizabeth. He had had his boys, since their divorce. Lizzie was three then, and a cutie-pie! Don had bi-weekly visitation with her, and Jenna most always went with him the thirty miles to pick her up. Don went religiously. He was not allowed to know where Corrie lived, and had to meet her in a parking lot. Jenna was new to all of this, and believed Don when he told her, it was all because of something Corrie had done. She now knew, that Don had been abusive to her also, and that was the real reason for the secrecy!

Whenever they had picked Lizzie up, the first thing they did was give her a decent meal. After visiting with her siblings, Jenna would put her in a warm tub. That night, Jenna was going to give her a bath. She took her in the bathroom, and started to undress her. What she saw made her gasp! The poor baby had bruises and belt-buckle marks, all up and down her right side! There were perfect, obvious belt-buckle imprints on her ribs, back, and buttocks. Jenna could see, she had been beaten. She called for Don. He came in and got quite upset. Jenna told him that she was reporting this, whether he wanted to, or not! After bathing her, and dressing her for bed, she prepared cookies and milk, and told all of the children to stay here, in the family room, that the police were coming, to talk to them. "Don't be afraid, kids. We just need to talk to them about something." "You guys can watch a movie, and stay up a while, if ya want."

Jenna went into the living room and called the police. She no more got child abuse out of her mouth, and two police cruisers pulled in the driveway! They were very polite, but concerned. They asked questions, we answered. They asked to talk to Elizabeth, Don called her, and they asked her questions, and had her pull her nightgown aside, and show the marks. The police asked if we wanted to press charges. Jenna let Don answer, and he replied, "Hell yes." We were awarded emergency, temporary custody that night, and decided that was it. Time to file for permanent custody! Lizzie was home to stay, from that night forward.

Other than regular sister squabbles, Lizzie and Nichole got along well. Having all these siblings was new for Nichole! Not only must she share her belongings, but, Mom's time and attention, too! They even shared a bed, until we built-on and provided more space for the throng! Jenna can admit, Nichole was somewhat of a spoiled brat, being the only child, and doted on by Grandparents so much!

We got full custody of Lizzie. Jenna had hired a good attorney, who is still her attorney, to this day. He has never lost her one case. The custody battle, was NO battle! The evidence was on our side,(on Elizabeth's side) and Corrie couldn't put up much of a fight. Jenna'd sure like to fight her! Do to her what she did to Fawn's boyfriend.

Jenna felt that she had always been willing to stick-up for Don, even fight his wars. But, she felt awfully unappreciated, unloved. Don's birthday was close to the Fourth of July, so every summer, Jenna threw him a hog roast. It was a lot of work, but fun, in the end! Jenna's husband all but forgot her birthdays. What with all the kids, parents, friends, and Don, it felt like she was throwing a party for someone, every month! One year, she threw a fit about having no party, no present, attention, not even a frigging card! Don said, "Hold your jets, I'll be right back!" He came back in the door, threw her an envelope, and Jenna thought, Wow. He sure put a lot of thought in this! On the card it said, May The Lord Richly Bless On Such An Occasion. Now, Don was not a church goer, didn't really have a religion that Jenna knew of. She told him, "Gee, thanks, hon. You sure perused the card rack well!" Don hated it when she used "big" words. Said she watched too much TV! Yes, Don, she had graduated past Romper Room.

That's why Steve's attention meant so much to Jenna. It was kind of like, throwing a life raft to a drowning person!

THE ROOT OF ALL EVIL

Before that fateful summer, it had been a life-changing and unusual spring. Jenna and her parents had almost always known that there was something wrong with her mentally. She could experience drastic mood changes, from pleasant, even-tempered, a girl with much energy, to a sullen, extremely depressed, angry girl, with little to no energy! She had never seen little green men, or heard voices in her head, but the changes in mood swings were dramatic! Over the years, she had had therapy, of many different kinds. Psychiatrists, psychologists, counselors, and none of these so-called professionals were ever able to diagnose what was wrong, or prescribe the correct medicine for it. When one has these drastic mood swings, they usually only seek help when depressed. When you swing to the other side of the void, one feels great! Creative, energetic, full of ideas! A lot of people also experience some darker parts of this side, which can include spending more money than they actually have access to, or not being able to relax or sleep, due to the million thoughts invading their ultra-active mind. Jenna has experienced these things also, but she would push these problems aside, as the better parts totally over-shadowed these! It was SO much better than sleeping all the time, thinking you had no purpose for being. It affected her relationships, school work, and general outlook on life.

It was difficult, if not impossible, to properly diagnose or research medical background of someone who had been adopted. If Jenna had a dollar for every medical form that she had had to mark, "unknown", on the background part, she would own her own shrink!! She had always known she was adopted. Her parents had never felt the need to lie, or hide it from her. Jenna was actually proud of this! Her biological mother had given her up, before she was even born, put into an orphanage after birth, and she had been hand-picked by her adoptive parents, at six weeks. Jenna's older brother and later, younger sister were all adopted. Her parents were unable to conceive, and God gave them us.

Jenna had always been curious about her history. Ethnicity, if she looked like anyone, what her medical background was. She wasn't looking for parents! She had those! The BEST. Besides, rotten times or not, if she could be given away, like a Goodwill donation, she wanted nothing BUT information!

There was a girl Jenna worked with, that most every day sat with her, at the break table, for cigarettes. One day she admitted to being adopted also, (like it was a damned crime!) and said she knew of a woman who would help find birth parents, for no fee. Not only did it sound very interesting to Jenna, it was also in her price range!! Chris said that she had had this information for a long time, but couldn't work-up the courage to call! She didn't want to hurt her parent's feelings. Jenna can understand that. But, she feels that the parents need to cut the kid a break! They weren't abandoned puppies, left in a fricki'n basket, on the porch! Whether adopted or not, every HUMAN should have access to their medical history. What? Wait until something catastrophic happened, and their history was a vital answer to their recovery? Respect a person's right to know. Information that most take for granted! A child does not ask to be born. Or, given away like pants that the dryer shrunk.

Chris gave her the number. Jenna had the next day off work, as she had a Dentist appointment. So, as soon as that was over, she was calling this woman, and hopefully be on her way to a prescription that would cure this see-saw shit. She told Don, he could have cared less, and she called her Mom, who wished her the best of luck. Mom was secure in the fact, that SHE was her Mom. Jenna had lain awake last night, deciding what she would say to this woman, even (silently) practicing. She felt like she was boning-up for mid-terms! In a way, she was. This was probably one of the most important tests of her life.

Jenna called the woman, who was very kind, explained her situation, and Edith told her that it shouldn't be that hard to do, as Jenna had a lot of the information needed. Jenna gave her home and work phone numbers, and told her to call Anytime! Edith said that it shouldn't take that long, and she would call, as soon as she knew. It only took two days! When Edith told Jenna that the woman didn't live that far away, Jenna was quite relieved to know she could drive to her house, in a relatively short time. Jenna thanked Edith profusely, and told her she had helped her, more than she knew.

Jenna took the day after the next off work, stopped at an Irish Pub, on the way, where one of her best friends bar-tended. And, of course she needed to calm her nerves with a beer! She looked up the phone number in the book, called on the pay phone, asked the woman who answered if that's who this was, and then, hung-up. Now Jenna had proof of her address, and that she was home. She finished her drink, and Syndo wished her luck, before she left, to meet this stranger.

It didn't take long to get there, and Jenna could see she lived in a small, non-descript house, on a side street. She took a deep breath, walked up to the door, knocked, and a short, older, replica of herself answered it. They both took a step backwards, shocked to witness an almost twin on the other side of the door. Jenna asked, "Does the date, September 24th, 1962 mean anything to you?" The woman swallowed deeply, then said, "You're my daughter, aren't you?" Jenna answered that she was, she just wanted to ask her a few questions. When she walked through the door, they hugged each other, for a few minutes. Jenna sat on a chair, and Zena introduced herself. Zena's husband joined them in the living room. Jenna asked if it was alright if she smoked, and Zena replied, "Sure! I smoke too!" They both lit up. Through out the time she spent there, she noticed that Zena had a definite problem with smoking. She would chain smoke, with inter-mittent puffs on a breathing machine. They talked for close to an hour, and Jenna found out that Zena had many mental difficulties.

She said that she was paranoid, schizophrenic, and manic-depressive, which is now called, bi-polar disorder.She had been institutionalized a few times, had tried committing suicide a few times, and was on a lot of medications. Jenna told her that she had some mental problems herself, and now she could go to her Doctor's, tell them she had proof of her disease; and finally get the proper help! Zena didn't offer much else concerning her background, couldn't even remember who Jenna's father (sperm donor) was, but, Jenna didn't really care. She got what she came for! And saw that she did look like Zena. She told Zena that she had Grandchildren, she would send pictures. By the time Jenna left, she could tell Zena was getting a bit freaked out, by all of this.

On the way home, Jenna's neighbor's owned a florist shop, and she stopped and ordered Zena a big bouquet of spring flowers, that were to be delivered tomorrow. She wasn't congratulating the woman for being her "mother", but thanking her for the useful information. She also sent her an envelope containing her Girl's photos in it, which were sent back, unopened. Her Loss. They had a great set of Grandparents. That was the last Jenna ever saw, or had anything to do with Zena.

Jenna was a Sun Worshipper. She laid out whenever possible. Don had built a rear deck on their house, and they had bought some nice patio furniture for it. The cushions and umbrella matched their new house siding, that Don had also put-on. They had also, recently built on a family room, and master bedroom with a walk-in closet. The added bonus of this, was the new attic, that ran from the old roof, to under the new one! It had the room needed for all of their storage. Before building the addition, he had also replaced most of the old windows, with new, double-paned glass. What a heating bill difference! Jenna learned early on that there was a BIG difference in Steve and Don's carpentry skills!! Steve couldn't hang a picture without assistance. Don's hands were good with wood. Steve's hands were good with skin.

MISPLACED TRUST

Jenna had a hard time trusting men. "But, you know I Luv Ya, Baby!!" Yah, ok. Maybe that's why she cheated. She'd hurt them, before they could hurt her! Hell, who knew for sure? She was no professional, not that she trusted them much, either. Jenna knew where most of this distrust came from. She hadn't known Steve long, when she told him what had happened to her. She wanted him to understand why she jumped at noises behind her, and why she insisted on sticking up for herself, taking care of things herself. The last thing Jenna wanted was some big, macho, man, sticking his nose where it didn't belong, throwing his weight around, trying to impress her with his manly prowess! She had bartended for years, and knew that most of the time, you didn't even have to get physical, intelligent but firm, verbal skills were usually all it took. Most of the trouble makers were drunk, anyhow! Drunk and or, stupid. A lot of the people in Jenna's life had been intelligently challenged. She had always felt smart, although she did question her common sense at times! In school, if she applied herself, she could do the work, and pass the damned tests. But, it was more important then, to get wasted, and laid! Part of the problem, was being from Small Town, U.S.A. And, The Wrong Side of The Tracks. The notion was, that if you grew up here, or poorer than most, you had limited intelligence. This generally came from those who had the right last name, and therefore thought their shit didn't stink! Most of these hoitey-toities lives never amounted to much, either.

There was one man in Jenna's life, who tried to keep her from having a productive future. He came damn close to succeeding! In 1984, right after Jenna left her first husband, Jenna had a devastating thing happen to her. Jenna and her first husband lived on a military base, with their daughter, Nichole. When their marriage broke-up, she moved to Michigan. She did not want anyone to say, she had tucked her tail between her legs, and ran home to Mommy and Daddy's! She rented a house right down the street from her Aunt. Her Aunt worked for a company that assembled products, and they told her she could do this at home. Jenna could earn money, and stay home and raise Nichole! She worked in her garage, and made enough to survive. Any spare time she had, she cleaned! Jenna had always been a neat freak, so, she cleaned walls, and woodwork, and cupboards. She put her plants and personal items around, and tried to make it feel like home.

Jenna started to date a guy she had met at her cousin's Graduation Party. She was actually starting to have fun again! Sandy and Nichole got along just fine, and that was definitely a good thing! She felt like she was pulling her life back together. Her split with Bruce had been really hard, as he was Jenna's first love, and Nichole's father. Laughing and joking around were becoming easier for her now. Love making was becoming easier and more enjoyable, with Sandy's love and patience.

That August, Sandy had a house party and of course, she was invited! Jenna hired a neighborhood woman to babysit, and she rode with friends to his house. Jenna needed to be home by midnight, as the babysitter had Church in the morning. Sandy discovered his car was blocked in, so Jenna decided to walk. It was a warm, summer night, and it was only about six blocks! She was almost home, when she heard footsteps behind her. Jenna would stop, they would stop. She'd start, they would. Now, Jenna was aware of her beer buzz, but she hadn't heard things! She stopped and looked behind her, but saw no one. Jenna was getting more freaked out and curious about this, as it continued. The buzz gave her enough courage, to stop, turn around, put her hands on her hips, and shout, " I know someone's there. I hear you. Step-out, and show yourself!" Nothing. Silence. She knew she hadn't imagined it!

Jenna turned around and hurried home. Most of her lights were on, so, in she went, checked on Nichole, paid the sitter, and watched her walk home. Jenna made a cup of tea, and opened the front door to let in the cool, night air, as it was so stuffy in here. Just then , her girlfriend, who had also been at the party, stopped to see if she had got home ok. Jenna finds that so ironic now! They said their good-by's, and Jenna left to go back in the door. She was on the top step when she turned to wave, and hear her friend beep her horn, good-by.

As she turned back, to go in the door, she felt hands, shoving her hard, pushing her in through the screen door. She barely had enough time to open it! Jenna was pushed across the room, into a wall. It knocked the air out of her! Not to mention, the fear and sheer terror , was making it hard to breath. The stranger shut and locked the front door. That was the first time she got a good look at him. He was not a real, tall man, fairly regular looking, like the Boy Next Door. Not some toothless creep, like you would expect. He told her to be quiet, and she wouldn't get hurt. He took her by the hand, and walked her around the house, to check it out, and to make sure all doors were locked. Jenna knew he was looking to see if she also had any company. She sure wished she did!! When he got to Nichole's bedroom, she stopped. He practically had to drag her, to get through the door. Jenna told him, "My baby is sleeping, and I don't want to disturb her!" He smiled an eery smile, and said, "Oh, let me see!" He rubbed his hands together in glee. Jenna noticed he had a feminine, high-pitched voice. That was the one time Jenna began to fight him, for all she was worth! She pushed him, with all her might, trying to get away from Nichole's door. He open-palm smacked her across her cheek and jaw, and she saw stars. He quietly walked through the bedroom door and looked in the crib, where a sleeping Nichole lay. She stayed sleeping. He came back out the door, and shut it. Jenna began offering him what ever he might be there to take. Her cheap stereo, her TV, jewelry, (Including the wedding rings from Bruce, that meant nothing to her now!) even the small amount of cash she had. He just chuckled, and told her to get on the couch. It was then, Jenna realized what he was really there for! She stopped, took off her own pants, and said, "Fuck me, and leave." He proceeded to finish undressing her. Jenna must have made a sound he didn't care for, because he gagged her with her own bra. She silently prayed, that he wouldn't take her life, and that Nichole would sleep through this, and stay out of this weirdo's way!! Thank the Good Lord, she did. He raped her. Jenna wanted to keep her eyes closed, but she looked him square in the eye, memorizing his features. When he finished with this, he rolled her over and attempted to sodomize her. This really frightened Jenna, as her and Bruce tried this once, and it had been too painful. She felt no pain, little discomfort even, as his penis was thumb size!! Later, she thought he had probably been teased about this, and maybe this was why he had turned to this! He finally was finished with her. She walked him to the back door, naked, and quickly showed him out. He ran out through the back yard.

Jenna made sure the door was locked, before she crumpled to the floor, sobbing her heart out. Directly above her, on the kitchen wall, was the telephone. She got up on her knees, grabbed the receiver, and dialed Sandy's number. She should have called the police first, but, she needed to hear his voice. Jenna barely croaked out rape, and Sandy and a carload of his buddies pulled in. Sandy came in, and the other guy's took off to look for this creep. Jenna fell into his arms, sobbing uncontrollably. He went and checked on Nichole, and brought her a robe to put on. They then called the police. Then Jenna called her Aunt, let her know what was happening, and asked her to watch Nichole while she went to be examined. Jenna knew from watching cop shows, what she should do afterwards. Not shower, and wash away evidence, and leave everything else alone, because of possible fingerprints.

Jenna spent most of the night at the local hospital, being checked-out, and having a rape kit done. They took lots of pictures, and even scraped under her nails. She had already made the determination to catch, and fully punish this sicko!! While they did all of this, Jenna was quiet. She was saying silent prayers of Thanks, for keeping her

Baby safe, and saving her life. She felt SO incredibly vile!! Like she needed ten showers, with sandpaper used as a washcloth! Sandy and friends gave her a ride back to her Aunt's house, where Jenna thankfully showered , and then fell into an exhausted sleep. Jenna was never able to walk in that house, again. She imagined him still there. In fact, for years to come, she saw his face everywhere. Jenna turned more and more to alcohol, to help her sleep, and help her forget that night. Alas, nothing she did could erase that face from her memory. It made everything about her life difficult, made her feel hopeless, useless. It even made her feel like she wasn't fit to be around her own daughter, he had made her feel so dirty!

The road of self-destruction had begun. Her self-esteem was nil, and her once plucky self-confidence was gone. Her parents tried to help, but they were as confused about this, as she was!! Jenna should have gotten some serious counseling then, but did not even realize this. She didn't think anyone would WANT to talk to her! Her trust had been destroyed, she may never be able to get close to anyone again.

This was a large piece of baggage that she carried around, for years to come. She carried a little with her, to this day.They did catch him, and he a got a 40 to 100 year sentence, on her charge, alone! But, Jenna still worried that he may get paroled, someday.

FALLING FAST

Jenna had had this feeling before. She was falling in love. At first, all she had wanted was a way out! She knew she couldn't support her girls, and afford a place for them to all live, on her salary alone. Steve was a good choice in many ways. He was no rocket scientist or Bill Gates, by far! He was only a factory worker, but a hard worker. Jenna wished he had more ambition. Steve had lots of ideas, but was such a procrastinator! The most important thing to Jenna, was that he had no ex-wife, or children from a previous relationship. Therefore, no competition. He had only really ever talked about one ex-girlfriend, Karen. He called her, "Stupid Karen." It was obvious, it hadn't ended well. Jenna knew she didn't have the right to feel jealous. She was the one who was married, for God's sake!! Neither of them were exactly virgins! Sex between the two of them, was intense. Sex with Don, was pretty much a snooze-fest. Jenna just wished Steve gave better kisses! Jenna had always prided herself on her wet, open-mouthed, involved kisses. Steve kissed with his mouth closed. It was kind of like kissing a mannequin! Jenna figured it was embarrassment over his teeth. Why didn't she surmise then, if he hadn't taken the time to care for his teeth, how could she expect him to care for a relationship? But, since she had always had a problem with impatience, she didn't take the time to put all of these signs together. Never had. She just wanted a way out!

Jenna spent every Friday evening with Steve and his family. They met them at the local VFW Hall. They had a Taco Night, also.

Mexican food had always been her favorite, and, hey, she didn't have to cook! Steve's family seemed so nice at first; she enjoyed spending time with them. She should have seen the evident "Momma's Boy" signs, by now! What's that old saying? Love Is Blind. Jenna was so busy trying to keep her marital status a secret, that she missed, or ignored them.

Jenna and Steve were at that, all-consuming, gushy, wide-eyed kind of affection, or infatuation, of early relationships. That, "I can't wait to get you out of here, and tear your clothes off", kind of feeling. They even had a waitress comment about their inability to order, as they were too busy, gazing into each other's eyes! Jenna did not plan on falling in love, but, it had happened anyhow!

Jenna had started to bring her youngest daughter, on these outings. In hindsight, she now realizes how wrong this was. Even if she did not want to leave her home with CJ, she should not have been a part of Jenna's cheating. On her own father! Charlise knew that things were bad at home, between her Mom and Dad. Jenna had tried to explain to her, how she was going to leave the house soon. But, that Charlise would always be with Mama, and Nichole, and she would still see her Daddy, often. Jenna and Don fought all the time now, and she had made a vow to never have a home with violence in it, again! Jenna's daughter's had always been the center of her world, the reason for her existence, she just didn't show them this enough. Unfortunately, children did not come with a "How To" book! Jenna hopes, that Charlise will forgive her, for making her keep this secret.

During this time, Jenna and Steve were falling madly in love. It was getting more and more difficult to keep her happiness from Don. A close friend of her's, would bitch at Jenna for throwing away all that she had with Don. She knew better than anyone, what she had with him! The decent part of him. Her girlfriend, and most people didn't know about the bad stuff. Why Jasmine had left, Charlise's molestation, and that Jenna had never really dealt with the insecurity involving the rape.

Halloween was approaching, and Jenna was busy making sure all of the children had costumes. Some she bought, and some she put together with things she found. Jasmine was gone now. Another family with bi-racial children, had adopted her this summer. Don had just woke-up one morning, gotten over whelmed by all the work and responsibility, and shouted, "Get the nigger out of my house!" Jenna tried to tell the agency, that she would leave Don, and raise Jasmine herself. They wanted her in a two parent family. Jenna was devastated. She suffered a minor breakdown, after Jazzy left. If she couldn't be a good Mom, she was nothing.

One night, Jenna and Steve had been out, when they pulled into his driveway, stopped the car, and Jenna started to cry. Steve reached over, and brushed the hair from her face. Jenna apologized for bawling, and told him, "You know, you really frighten me." Steve was surprised at this. "Why, on Earth are you afraid of me, Sweetheart?" "I'm not afraid of you. Of falling in love with you." Steve grinned and responded, by grabbing her close, and telling her that he loved her too! They embraced each other tightly, and kissed a long, loving kiss. It was, by far, the best hug Jenna had ever felt. They both ended it a little teary eyed, and grateful to have found one another.

Jenna was getting ready for Halloween. The kid's costumes, decorating the house, helping the kid's stuff a scarecrow man, and shopping for candy to hand out. This would be the first time Nichole would meet Steve, as they were going Trick-or-Treating with him. Nichole now lived with her Paternal Grandmother, after moving from Arizona, where she had lived with her father. Nichole had been miserable living with Don and the boys, so, Jenna gave Bruce custody. Signing those papers nearly killed her! Bruce had promised them both, that she would be happy with him. She was miserable there too! When Jenna told Nichole about Steve, she was typical Nichole! "Mother!" "You're not even done with one, and you're hooked up with another!" "Isn't that what they say, going from the frying pan, into the fire?" "'Haven't you had enough of men's crap?" Jenna really couldn't say much in return. She knew she was right!

All in all, they enjoyed Halloween Night. Charlise was Snow White and Nichole was Cleopatra. Jenna had told Steve about hers and Nichole's Manic-Depressive illness, and how it would affect one's life, if they were not properly medicated. Well, Nichole was medicated, and she still managed to show her true colors, that night!

Jenna realized that Nichole was actually taking the disappointment she had for her Mother, out on things in general. She later explained this to Steve, how Nichole was leery of "new" men in her Mom's life, as, so far, they hadn't turned out so good!

When Nichole lived with her dad in Ohio, he took her to a Psychiatrist, that was a junkie, and crazier then all of her patients, put together! She wore dark, clown make-up, and was absolutely NO help to Nichole. The day Jenna went to court, for the charges her ex and his Bimbo, were making about Don and his boys, was an awful day for Jenna. Her Mom had rode with her and Don, as she was allowed to see Nichole in the Court House that day. Jenna was not. To know that she was right around the corner and just down the hall from her, and yet not be able to touch her ,hold her, even talk to her was terrible.

The crazy lady testified; after being late for court, as she "got lost." She was so stoned, it was hard for her to pronounce words, and she even said that Nichole was not easy to like! Jenna stood up and shouted, "I like her!!" The judge was even disgusted by her behavior. Jenna won the case, and was given un-supervised visitation. The Judge was such a kind woman; she knew how much Jenna was struggling financially with no Child Support, that she even helped pay for Nichole's much needed orthodontia!! That showed Jenna that there were still some decent folks on this planet.

Nichole's father, step-mother, and Paternal Relatives, denied her having a Mental Illness, as it had(s) this stigma attached, that anyone suffering from one, is straight-jacket, institution ready, nuts!! So, instead of dealing with the DISEASE like mature adults, send her to an even more disturbed Doctor!! As parents, we need to admit to sometimes being wrong. As patients, we need to "fire" Doctor's who displease or anger us, and we all need to show the kind of graciousness the Judge did, that day.

Jenna foolishly followed her heart again. It had led her in the wrong direction before, why was she acting rashly and going in the path it led? How could she ever give her Girls advice, when she didn't even follow it? If you can answer this, I'll pay ya.

IN PREPARATION

Jenna worked with a girl named Maria, at the Nursing Home. They had become fast friends, in a short amount of time. One of the things they had in common, was a good sense of humor. Maria had told Jenna that she lived in a Trailer Court, in the next town over. She said that the trailer next to hers was up for rent, and the rent was decent. Jenna knew that the Park had a questionable reputation, but, it would only be temporary, and it was in her price range. Besides, by this point, she was pretty much desperate!

In the meantime, her and Don's marriage was going down hill fast. Just last weekend, Jenna had insisted that they go out tonight. It had been ages since they had done anything without the children, and Jenna was still clinging to the hope that things would get better! She had picked up a second job, at a restaurant/pub, where she had worked at once before. Once she had paid for his DWI, her savings were depleted, and she knew she would need money for all the deposits! They went to dinner, at her place of employment, (where she got a discount), and she paid with last nights tips! Afterwards, Jenna wanted another drink, so they went to a Tavern, close by. Oh course, he had to have one too! On the way home, Don ran a red light, and got arrested for DWI. He blamed Jenna for it; saying she was the one who wanted to go to the bar! He even got nasty with her at the Police Station, in front of the Cops! They looked at Jenna, with sympathy in their eyes.

Don served his three days, then came to her job at the Nursing Home, and took her car! After she had sold her Cutlass, Don bought a used Chevy from his boss. He got it for a low price, and it ran good, and looked decent. Jenna came out after work, and her car was missing! She instantly knew that Don had taken it. He had told her before, that what was hers, was his, and she wouldn't leave with his stuff! Jenna called her Dad, and he gave her a ride. The very, next day, Steve took her shopping for a CLUB. This was a device that clamped onto the steering wheel, and kept anyone from driving or stealing it. This really pissed Don off! It gave Jenna piece of mind, knowing that her car would be where she left it!

Jenna found out there was a $250.00 deposit on the trailer they were going to rent, and she didn't have it! Steve didn't either. He didn't want to ask his mommy and daddy for it, so Jenna had to borrow it from hers. That was to become a habit with Steve. She found out later, he didn't like to borrow from relatives, as he never paid them back! And, they knew it. Jenna would work three job's(she had) in order to pay back what she owed. That was why her parents did not have a problem with lending her money! What makes a man feel that his loans are greater, or more difficult to pay back, than a woman's? As far as Jenna was concerned, women were just more respectful.

Jenna had already decided what belongings she was going to take, and what she would leave behind. Don could keep his furniture! The bed, for example. Jenna had had to share it with him all these years, knowing it had been him and his ex-wife's bed, also! It made her skin crawl, just to think of it!! Don and his third wife probably still have it, knowing the Cheap Bastard. Let her sleep with the ghosts of wives and lovers past. The last time her and Steve slept in it, Steve left them a "present" on the mattress.

The last night Don slept in the house, before Jenna left him, she had been out, with Charlise, looking at the trailer. When she pulled back in, she noticed that his truck was still in the driveway, and the neighbors were having a bonfire. That meant that he was rip-roaring, and informing the neighbors about what a bitch she was! Let him. They got undressed, and ready for bed, and Jenna let Charlise snuggle in with her. They weren't in the bed thirty seconds, when the sliding door opened, and here stumbled Don. He went to Jenna's side of the bed, slurringly asked her, "Where ya been, ya whore?" Jenna pretended to stay asleep. Don then grabbed her arm, and jerked her, trying to wake her up. Jenna snatched her arm from his, and angrily said, "We're sleeping! Go back to your drinking buddies." He grabbed her by the hair this time, and pulled her from the bed. He then gave her a mighty shove, knocking the wind out of her, and putting her across the room. Now, she was pissed! If the drunken asshole wanted a fight, he would have one. Jenna just did not want to have it, in the same room Charlise was in! She turned to go into the family room, when he grabbed her wrist, turned her back around, and bitch-slapped her across the face. Jenna was almost grateful that he did this, as she knew that one would leave a good bruise! Jenna could still leave the Wimp, and she would (hands down) win the divorce case! She even said, "Good one!" under her breath, he shoved her again, and threatened to finish this off, when Jenna felt a wire hanger, on the floor under her feet, and she bent down and grabbed it. The next time he went to punch her, she was ready. She swung back, and hit him in the head, hearing it go, "Wwwwhack!!!!" Don stopped, looked at her in shock, and said, "Ooooh!!! You bitch!!!" Jenna took off running towards the bathroom, away from Charlise, and the only room in the house with a lock. Don was right behind her. He shoved her inside, and shut the door. Jenna took a quick glance in the mirror, and saw that her eye was already beginning to swell shut. Don saw it, too. He then grabbed her by the nose, began to twist it, and said, "I'll make it so no one else likes this pretty face!" He twisted it until it started to gush blood, and Jenna heard a "SNAP!!" She guesses this freaked him out, because he then quit. All the time he was beating her, Jenna had yelled for help, quite a few times. All three of his kids were supposedly asleep, but she was hoping someone could stop him! No one came to her rescue. She decided, right then, she was done doing for them, too!

Don got ready for work, then left. As soon as he left, Jenna called the Police. When the cruiser pulled in the driveway, so did Don's truck! He probably knew he was in deep shit, and didn't want to be arrested at work. It wasn't hard to convince them she had been beaten, when her eye was swollen shut, and she looked like a freaking chipmunk!! They took Don away , in cuffs, and he ended up doing a 90 day sentence.

Steve, more or less, moved in. Don's kids went to stay with an Aunt, as Jenna sure was not responsible, ANYMORE. Don had to pay all of the household bills, while incarcerated. All but food. When he canceled the dumpster, she put the bags of garbage in CJ's room. Garbage deserves garbage. Jenna began to pack, in earnest. Her and Don owned the little house next door, and used it for a rental property. It almost paid their house payment! Of course, Jenna went to the renter's and told them to pay her, from now on. So, while Don made the house payment, Jenna got the rent! It was all SO convenient for Steve! A nice house to live in, a woman in your bed every night, NO BILLS, no responsibilities, and no real commitment. Even Steve's friends told him how good he had it! Jenna later realized what he really wanted was Mommy #2!!

Jenna packed and took everything that had been purchased with HER credit cards! She was nice enough to leave a tiny cooler, on the floor, in place of the side-by-side!!

THE BIG MOVE

Jenna moved in January. Not the best time to move! It was extremely cold, and there was about a foot of snow on the ground. Steve had borrowed the truck from work, and they had managed to fit all of her belongings in one load. Before she left the house, her and Steve removed every light bulb they could find. She had been savings the burnt out bulbs for months, and was now replacing the good with the bad. Steve was quite tall, so he even took the bulbs out of the chandeliers! Jenna wanted Don to walk in, flip on the light switch, and when nothing happened, continue on to the next light, and the next, and the next!! Jenna and Steve laughed so hard, just imagining the look of consternation, crossing Don's face! She wanted one last laugh.

Steve's younger brother, and his friend Billy, were helping with the move. They all shared a laugh over the light bulb deal! Besides the rotten weather, Jenna really regretted moving in the winter. She had lots of bulbs and perennials that she had wanted to dig-up and take with her. She had spent her own money and effort, to plant the damn things. Oh well. The ground was frozen now. The one thing they forgot, meant a lot to Jenna. She almost cried when she realized they had left it. It was a young, fig tree, in a pot she had just purchased for it. Jenna's Mom had given the tree to her, and she had bought the pot and re-planted it. She knew Don would kill it. Like he had their marriage.

Jenna had separated the boxes that were going to the trailer, from the boxes that were being stored, beforehand. When they got to her Brother's house, they all helped carry boxes, downstairs, to the basement. There were only a few pieces of furniture that were to be stored, also. She handed out, Thank You's, and kisses, before they went to the trailer. They moved the rest of it into the trailer. It was nighttime because they had to wait to move, as they all had worked that day. Needless to say, they were all pooped! She would wait 'til another day to move things where she really wanted them.

They didn't have a bed yet, as Jenna had left Don his, nest of fools, and Steve's king size water bed was too much work for a temporary place. The next day, the rented one from the local Rent-A-Shop. Charlise's regular bed was a set of bunk-beds, which were too big for her bedroom, so Jenna put the fold-out love-seat in her room. It all worked out fine. Jenna did her best to make it feel homey and comfortable. She thoroughly cleaned, hung pictures, put her knick-knack around, and hung her own curtains. Jenna took the guilt she felt for taking Charlise from the only home she had ever known, out on dirt! Cleaning was a form of therapy for her. They all seemed to be content, living here. Come spring, Jenna planted flowers around the trailer, and the neighbors commented on how nice this was. Steve's attitude was, "He worked 40 hours a week! As long as helped with the bills, the domestic stuff, was women's work!" Well, Jenna always worked at least, 40 hours a week herself! If a job didn't work out, or wasn't enough money, she got another! And, maybe another! And still managed a house, kids, yard, and spoiled man! Jenna had always been taught, No one owed her a living, that if she wanted to make it, she had to work for it. She had tried to impress this on her kids, too. Steve would help with the trips to the Laundromat. Charlise looked forward to this day! For some reason, she loved the Laundromat.

During the year that they lived there, Jenna made surface-friendships with a few neighbors. Most were strange enough, indeed "Trailer Trash", but Jenna made an effort to be decent. The worst part about living there, was that their trailer sat so close to the railroad tracks. The trains were quite loud, especially at night. That's when they ran the most, horn blowing and all! The vibrations about shook you from the bed! This seemed the perfect time for sex. Charlise couldn't hear the moans and groans from her Mom's room, and if they woke her up, she could just say, "Damn trains."

Nichole would come visit Jenna and Charlise, every other weekend. She would either crash with her sister, or on the couch. Jenna wished she had her own bedroom too, but Nichole didn't seem to mind. They all got along well, and had quite a few good times together. Jenna desperately wanted Nichole back for good! Don and the boys were history, so she knew this was a big, point in her favor. She still had to be patient, and wait until her divorce was final. Her first set of in-laws could be just as picky as her second! (Wasn't that a Law?) Jenna wanted Nichole to be happy. She tried to keep things around that Nichole liked. First: there was the chameleon. He lived in a glass aquarium and ate crickets, you had to purchase from the Pet Store, and toss into him. They came home in a paper bag, which had to be emptied quickly, as they would chew their way free! Steve and Charlise went one night, and got the crickets while Jenna was at work, and when she got home, there were cups, placed upside down, all over the trailer. She asked Steve, "What's with the cups?" Charlise put her hand over mouth, to stifle a laugh, and Steve said, "The crickets escaped, and we're trying to capture them." They all three helped locate and confine escaped crickets, laughing all the while! What a hoot!! That scene would have won, "America's Funniest Home Video."

The next pet Nichole had, was a Guinea Pig. J'ose. He was not Jenna's favorite creature, that's for sure! He was also kept in the glass aquarium. Jenna had never seen an animal shit so much!! Which drew flies, by the hundreds. Eat, sleep, poop. Trying to get Nichole to clean the cage, was like trying to get a man to admit guilt. But, Nichole loved her J'ose, so , he stayed.

Ok, so the neighbors were weird, the trains were loud, and the Guinea Pig drew flies. She was free! And starting a new life with Steve.

MOO'VIN ON UP –
TO THE BIG HOUSE

After Jenna, Steve, and Charlise lived there for eight months, they started looking for a different place to rent. Any place away from these frigging railroad tracks, would be an improvement! They eventually found a nice, big farm house, in the country, just outside of Steve's hometown. The rent was steep, but , once again Jenna saved the day. She got her and Don's rental property in the divorce settlement, and the money she received in rent, paid most of her and Steve's rent. It was a nice, three bedroom, two car garaged house in the country. Jenna tried to represent all of their tastes, when she decorated it. The five-acre property had several outbuildings, a large barn, and lots of grass to mow! The Landlord furnished the riding mower, and it took most of the day to do. They would often spend time in the barn, investigating it. It even had a playhouse, with electric outlets, that the Girl's could play in! At least, Charlise did.

Steve wasn't as glad to live there as Jenna was. He had always lived in town; Jenna had grown up in the country. She knew her kids had been through some rough times, and wanted them to run, laugh, have friends over, enjoy their youth, while they could! Once again, they moved in the dead-of-winter! They were so glad to be out of the trailer park, it was worth it! They were able to put Charlise's bunk-beds up, and Steve brought his waterbed from his parents. It was hard to find beds long enough for him! Jenna never had that problem, as she was so short! They never seemed to have a problem fitting together though. She finally got full custody of Nichole back, and they were happy here, a family. Both Girl's were ensconced in the local school district, and Jenna got involved as much as work would allow.

It wasn't long and Nichole found a stray cat on the property. It was hungry, and looking for affection. She went to her Mom and pleaded for the cat. She's so cold Mom! We'll get a litter box, and I'll even take care of it! The Landlord never has to even know, we'll hide her when they come. And so, Jett came into our home, our hearts. Jett had lovely long fur, and was Jet black. She was an excellent mouser, stayed outside 50% of the time, and one day she left half a rabbit on our doorstep. Maybe she felt she had to prove her worth to us, but, it was already too late.

Jenna's favorite part of the house, was the big, country kitchen. It had a double-oven, a dishwasher, plenty of cupboard space, and three large windows, for her plants to hang in. The only bad part of the room, was the white tiled floor. It always needed mopped! Jenna thought that was a small price to pay, for such a beautiful room! One good thing was it also had a mud- room, inside the back door, where the kids came in from school, and could hang up coats, and take off shoes before entering the rest of the house. Between the kitchen and the mud-room was a Laundry Room. The property also had a long clothesline that Jenna used in the warm months. The bathroom was next to that, and the Master Bedroom was off the bathroom. The whole house had many windows, that let the fresh air, and sunlight in. Jenna made sure they gleamed. The Living Room was at the front of the house, and it was carpeted in a lovely, forest-green pile. There was also a front porch, with a railing, that was perfect for Christmas decorations. The birdhouse outside the main kitchen window, was a favorite of Charlise's. Steve would lift her up, to fill it with seeds, as she couldn't reach it. The stairs were off the living room, and there were two, good-sized bedrooms upstairs. The Girl's each had their own space. It also had a large attic, off of Nichole's room, that they also enjoyed investigating.

All in all, it was a nice place to live. Jenna had agreed to marry Steve by then, and they had started to look for a place to buy.They had discussed this at length, and they both agreed they felt like they were just wasting money, paying rent, when they could put the money towards purchasing one. The next time the Landlord came to pick-up the rent, Jenna asked him, if he had ever considered selling. After biting their heads off, he almost whined to them, "I was born in this house! I wouldn't dream of selling it!" (He sold it, shortly after they moved.) Their house hunt began.

During the year that they lived here, Jenna's Mother's health began to decline rapidly. Her Mom, and her sister Fawn, had been estranged since Fawn had dumped Jasmine. Jenna and her Mom, had always been close; she was Jenna's best friend. They both knew Estelle would be gone soon. They talked about death often. Neither of them were afraid of it. They were both Born Again Christians, and knew that Heaven was a better place. One of their conversations was about Fawn, and about how much Estelle would like to see her, and hopefully repair things before "The End." Jenna realized how important this was to her Mom, so, she promised her she would try and find her. All they knew for sure, was that she lived on the East side, of the next big city. On her next day off work, Jenna drove to the East side, and stopped at an infamous corner bar. She started conversing with several patrons, and it didn't take long to find someone who knew Fawn. Jenna drank a beer with the attractive man, who had said he knew Fawn. He said he knew where she lived, and would go get her, if she wanted. They did not have a phone.He said his name was Bobby, that he'd be glad to go get her.He drank his beer, then left. It wasn't long, and Fawn came in the front door, almost screaming her name! "JENNA!!"" They gave each other a big hug, exchanged kisses, and sat down to talk. Jenna told her about their Mom, and she wanted them all to come to her house for Easter dinner. Fawn said that if her "piece of shit" car would make it to "The Boonies", she'd be glad to come! They gave each other their addresses and phone numbers (Fawn's work number) and said their good-byes. Jenna told Steve and the Girl's, and they were glad she was coming to see Grandma. The next thing Jenna did, was call her parents and tell them. Mom was relieved she was ok, and was excited to see her. They discussed Easter dinner at Jenna's , and that Fawn was coming. This was only a month away, so Jenna had a menu to plan!

Jenna made a Leg of Lamb, several side dishes, rolls, salad, dessert, and even bought a good, bottle of wine. And, of course had plenty of hot coffee on hand! Her parents were avid coffee drinks, as was Jenna. Steve hated it. More for them!

Jenna's parents arrived before Fawn did. They were all sharing hor d'oever's, and steaming cups of coffee, when Fawn pulled in. Hugs and kisses were passed around, many tears were shed, and they all enjoyed each other and the meal together. The day had gone very well, and Jenna was relieved to have made this wish possible for her Mom. They all agreed to keep in contact, and they did!

ANOTHER DAY, ANOTHER DOLLAR

When Jenna and Steve moved into the farm house, Jenna was working for a small, privately owned, commercial cleaning business. She had quit her other two jobs, as they were too far to drive. She mostly cleaned company's property, that was just being built. That meant everything from sawdust, to mud! She also cleaned a few offices. The biggest job she had was a new, steel mill, under construction, that was very close by. Jenna cleaned the construction trailers, that belonged to certain companies. She also cleaned the crews, gross, work restrooms. She had to wear a hard-hat on sight, and knee-high boots, because of the mud. The mud was unbelievable! It would suck the boots, right off your feet! It was hard, dirty work, but they needed the income, so, Jenna did it. She worked for this company for a about one year, the plant finished construction, and work was sparce. She still cleaned an occasional office, mostly the other new, steel plants corporate office building, around the corner from the mill. It wasn't as much money as before, so she was looking for a more, steady job. Steve was working for a factory that made car parts. Employment was a constant, revolving door, so Jenna told Steve to tell his boss that she was interested in a job. She had never worked in a factory before, but had never considered herself a Prima Dona, and didn't think any job was beneath her! As long as it put food on the table, and paid the rent, she was not picky. Two days later, his boss, Tim, called and hired her over the phone. Another hot, dirty, MONOTONOUS job! And factory work was SO gossipy. You probably spent more time with those people than you did your own family, and because of that, everyone there thought they knew your business! Jenna hadn't been there long, when her hands started to ache and fall asleep at night. She still managed to keep the house, though.

While Jenna and Steve lived there, they had a few parties at the farm house. Billy gave them a refrigerator he was no longer using. Steve put in the garage, and it worked out perfectly for parties. They had a Halloween party, complete with costumes, a keg of beer, and decorations. They also threw a surprise birthday party for a friend of they'res wife. They also had a few outside parties that summer. The yard was plenty big, and Jenna had nice, patio furniture. Everyone brought picnic-type food, and plenty of cold beer. At one of those parties, Steve's relatives were there, just sitting around, enjoying conversation, and each other's company. All of a sudden, out of the blue, Steve's Uncle's chair just collapsed from underneath him! Between giant guffaws of laughter, they made sure he was ok. They all got a long laugh, out of that one! Jenna had made friends with most of Steve's relatives, and had come especially close with his Uncle Neil and Aunt Loralyn. (He was the one on the ground now.) Her and Loralyn had been joking about how they had lost their cherries, long ago, and had grown a new fruit by now! From then on, no matter what occasion, Neil and Loralyn bought them something to do with cherries! It was always good for a laugh. Neil had even agreed to take the wedding photographs, as a gift. Too bad, only a few came-out ok. Or, was it?

Jenna really enjoyed living here. From feeding the birds, to hanging Christmas garland on the front porch. Feeling like a real family; that was the best. After Christmas that year, money had become very tight. Jenna's tenant was late on her rent, which made them late on they'res. They were living off of this rental income, and both of their factory salaries. The Girl's always needed something, and Jenna tried giving her divorce attorney a little, whenever she could. He knew he would get paid in full, as soon as Jenna had it, and had been pretty patient about it. Jenna asked her boss if she could take over the cleaning duties from the current crew, as she could use the extra income, and they weren't very good, anyhow! So, after working eight hours on the floor, she stayed and cleaned six offices, and two, big bathrooms. The other employees commented on the good job she was doing. Jenna knew they were not paying her near as much money, as they had the other crew, and she was doing the work of three people! Jenna's hands were getting steadily worse, and the pain was unbearable, at times. She stuck it out, as long as she could. At home, she was living on aspirin and Ben Gay, and simple things were getting harder to do. She would often get-up at night, leaving the room, to go and bawl, not wanting to wake Steve up. He was supportive, but he also knew how much they needed her paychecks! Nichole would say, "Just quit, Mom!" "We'll make it, we always do." Jenna hated for her Daughter's to see their Mom in such pain. Charlise's small Child Support helped, too bad Bruce didn't pay his! Jenna continued to work through the pain. Bills came first. That was the only real point of contention between her and Steve. Money. He thought if it was in his pocket, it was his to spend. Jenna eventually had to have him direct deposit his paycheck, into a joint account. After she made sure the bills were met, he could have the rest. Jenna had kids, she did not want to be a grown man's Mama!

WHOSE SETTLEMENT WAS IT ?

Jenna and Steve showed the rental property to a couple who worked with them, who were interested in buying. Jenna had decided she would sell the property, as it was too difficult having the house directly next to Don's. She knew that between renters, the house needed cleaning and painting, and she did not trust Don. While they were showing the property to their friends, Don came out holding a baseball bat. The four of them had been out back, in the woods, and were greeted with this sight when they came back up. After exchanging some unpleasant remarks, Don walked over and let his German-Shephard out of his kennel. Now, he probably would have attacked, but this dull knife forgot Jake used to be Jenna's dog, too!! After things calmed down, they all left, and Jeb and Carol decided against buying the house. Who could blame them, with a psycho neighbor?

Within the week, Jenna went to a local Relater's office to discuss the sale. God was smiling down on her, this day! When Jenna told the Relater about the house and property, his eyes lit-up and he said, "You know, I've been looking for a small house to use as a rental income." They continued their discussion, finally agreeing on a price. He wrote her a check, that very day! They agreed on a take-over date, they shook hands, and then Jenna turned and gave him a hug. "This is such a relief to me, sir!" "Now, I can pay some bills and get away from my ex." He remarked how it would be a good investment for him, and was glad to help.

As Soon as Jenna shared the good news with Steve and the girls, they all celebrated with a pizza and soft drinks, later Jenna and Steve with celebratory sex. The next weekend was Memorial Day, so Jenna and Steve planned a party on the rental property. They figured there would be enough people at the party, that if Don wanted to show-up, let him!

Jenna invited a few people from where she used to work, they both invited a few people from the factory, some of Steve's relative's, some of Jenna's, and each of their closest friends. The party was in the back yard, but the back door was kept open for access to the bathroom. It seemed there was no one home next door. They weren't missed. Don's picnic table was sitting on the property line, in the back yard.(The picnic table made from wood that Jenna had paid for.) They were enjoying each other's company, drinking some beers, and telling jokes. All of a sudden, Don's mother, Hazel, came stomping out the back door, demanding they give Don's picnic table back! There were more than a few people who wanted to tell her where to put the table, but, Jenna held up her finger, and said, "Fine Hazel. We will put the stupid table back." Hazel hesitated, expecting them to move the table immediately. Jenna was getting pissed. She almost shouted, "Give us a damn minute!" At that, Hazel turned and stormed back into the house. One of Steve's buddies smiled mischievously and said, " If they want it, they can have it!" At this, he turned away from the people seated across from him, unzipped his fly, and proceeded to whiz all over the top of the table. Pretty soon, every male at the party was pissing all over the picnic table!! Jenna commented on how that would be nice and sticky, after drying in the sun! They all laughed their asses off over that one. The party went until late, and they all said what a good time they had had. Jenna had invited one of her girlfriend's from the nursing home, who was always good for a laugh! Her name was Hahnna, and she was a hoot! When Hahnna told Jenna she was leaving, Jenna thanked her for coming and gave her a big hug. On the way to her car, that was parked out front, Hahnna cut-over to Don's yard and up on his rear deck. Jenna watched her pull her pants down and take a piss! When she was finished, she came down and met Jenna in the yard. Between the incident and the beers, they both fell to the ground, hugging and laughing hysterically!!

Because of the beating she took, Jenna knew from her lawyer, that she was destined to receive a decent settlement from her divorce from Don. She had decided early on that she wouldn't ask for alimony. Don had recently claimed a disability, and wasn't working currently. So, she knew that receiving the alimony was questionable.

But, she knew the rental property was worth something, and it wouldn't affect Don's kids. Jenna was asking way too little for it, she knew. She was more concerned with paying her lawyer and her credit cards off, not getting rich. The amount she had asked her Relater for was fairly low to begin with, and then he asked for another two thousand off because he said it needed a new roof. Jenna thought this was a scam, as there had never been any leaks or problems with it. It was impossible to ask Don, and Steve could barely tie his own shoes! In the end, she agreed and took the check.

First thing she did was pay her lawyer. Then she paid off three credit cards, paid ahead on their rent, bought Nichole a new bed and mattress,put $500.00 down on a Blazer her and Steve were buying, and put some in the bank for the wedding and their new house.Jenna's car had a rather simple radiator problem, but seeing how Steve was car incompetent, she eventually sold it to a guy she worked with. They found a Blazer they both liked. They were both Chevy people, and thought a 4-wheel –drive was the way to go. Of course, when they applied to purchase it, they were told that Steve had some overdrawn items on his past credit, that were complicating things. Jenna once again came to the rescue! She paid off his two bills and his father still had to co-sign. Not because of Jenna's credit, but Steve's. The first day they had the Blazer, they went up to the local bar for a drink to celebrate their purchase. They did not stay very long as they both had to work in the morning.When they got in front of the house, Steve stopped the truck. There was a good two feet of snow on the ground, and they thought it was a good time to check out the 4-wheel-drive.

They both grinned, and Jenna said, "Go for it, Hon!" So, they went four-wheeling through the yard! They only went in the part of the yard that they knew was flat, with nothing in their way. They both laughed like idiots, and had a blast! The next morning, they saw the deep tracks in the snow, and laughed all over again.

Jenna and Steve had been house shopping , all this time. Steve wanted to live in town, so Jenna only showed him newspaper advertisements of "town" houses that were for sale. They saw a few houses they liked, but of course, they couldn't buy anything that needed maintenance! Bless his heart, he wouldn't be any help with this! Jenna bought nothing for herself with this money. She sure deserved to, but was too busy taking care of other's needs.

FLAWED CLAWS

Jenna's hands were really getting bad. Her regular doctor had suggested she go to a specialist, that she probably had carpal tunnel syndrome. All she knew was, she needed relief! It had started to hurt up her arms and into her neck. She was up most nights with the pain and the numbness. Steve and the Girl's knew how bad it had gotten. Jenna continued work for as long as she could take it. Even simple tasks at home were getting difficult. Eventually, the specialist suggested surgery for both hands, and since that meant no work for a while, he gave her the name and number of a Worker's Compensation Lawyer. This was to cover the expense of the operations, and doctor bills, and to pay her for the time she would be off work. As soon as some of the other employees and the boss at work found out, rumors started to fly. Good old factory rumors! Everyone thinks they know your business. That comes from spending too much time together, Jenna thought. It wasn't one week after she informed the owner what was happening, and they "let Steve go." They fired him! He was one of their very, first employees! He drove truck for them, and had driven with faulty vehicles, through storms, over icy roads, to other, ill-serviced factories. Jenna always thought that Steve blamed her for this. He told her that he didn't, but he had known the owner's most of his life. Yet, one more thing her fiancé and future in-laws blamed her for. It was the factory's fault she got carpal tunnel, and it was their fault that Steve lost his job!

Jenna and Steve finally found a house, in the middle of all this. They were buying a house when neither of them had a job. Thank goodness Jenna had money in the bank from her settlement! Steve didn't have squat, and they both knew it. Fortunately, Steve was out looking for employment immediately. I'm sure Jenna's prodding helped. He had a new factory job, before they went to closing. Nichole and Charlise were out of school for the summer, so everyone was busy packing and cleaning. Nichole reminds her Mother of her complaining about the lifting, because of her hands!! Jenna also needed their help with the cleaning. They all pitched in.

Jenna and Steve had decided on a three bedroom , one and a half bath, two-story, one-car garage house, with a fenced in backyard. It was in town, of course, close to both schools, and directly across from a park. It was obviously an older house, one which they later found out was 140 years old! One of the first houses built in this town. The kitchen was an add-on, and neither of them were crazy about it, but the rest of the house fit. Including the price. In the half bath downstairs was a pull-up door that led to a staircase, that led to the basement. It was only a half basement, but a place to store the water heater, furnace, and them, if there was a tornado. There were two bedrooms upstairs, and a full bath. The master bedroom was fairly large and had a big, walk-in closet. The bedroom downstairs had no closet, but there was an extra closet in the hallway, upstairs. The downstairs bedroom was given to Nichole. Charlise had the room across from the upstairs bathroom.

The dining room had a wooden floor, and a nice chandelier. The living room did have a downfall, and that was the remnants of an old fireplace. The chimney was still intact, running up the wall, and beneath it was a brick square, where the fireplace itself used to stand. So, here was this useless obstacle in the middle of the living room. Jenna said they would work around it somehow. She immediately had future plans for the house and yard.

THE LAST MOVE— TOGETHER

On the last day at the farmhouse, the owner was there to check for the deposit return, and get the key. Now, on the day they took the house, the owner's wife was there, showing the house to Jenna, and checking for the last tenant's deposit. The woman was in a big hurry to rent the house to Jenna, as she knew Jenna had the $1400.00 deposit, and it was winter time and they spent winters in Florida. One thing she missed, that Jenna and Steve noticed right off, was a cracked window pane in the front window. Since she never said anything, they surmised it was of no consequence to her. When the owner did the final run-through, the cracked window was quoted as a broken window, and he found one pea sized black spot on the living room carpet. There was also worn linoleum underneath the washing machine, where it had leaked. They owned the washing machine, themselves. Jenna and Steve were told, they were not going to get their deposit back. They were dumbfounded! The only item that was their fault was the spot. Mighty damn expensive spot! Jenna was in tears, and Steve had his hands bunched-up and his teeth gritted. They were standing in the driveway with the owner, getting ready to leave, when the owner asked for the keys. Steve and Jenna gladly threw them at him.

Steve and Jenna went back to the house, picked up the girls, and went shopping. They were looking for the right color of paint, to paint the master bedroom, Charlise's bedroom, and Nichole's bedroom. They wanted a dark blue for the master bedroom, Charlise wanted pink, and Jenna was going to sponge paint blue and black splotches on a white background in Nichole's bedroom. Jenna also needed enough of the white to paint the half bath, too. They also picked up enough paint brushes and rollers to do the job. Jenna also bought a new shower curtain and some new curtains for Nichole's windows. Steve made sure they had ceiling paint, as this was his job, because of his height. After the ceilings were painted, Jenna and Nichole painted the rest, except for the places they couldn't reach. The left over pink paint was used on the main bathroom shelves. It turned out well. Jenna wanted to paint much more, but this would do for now.The next time she shopped, she bought a new mailbox and house numbers, as the old ones were in need of replacements. Steve helped her hang them. They were all moved in now, it was their new, and last home together.

As soon as the painting was done, Jenna had her hand operations. She was glad to have the relief, as the painting had been quite painful. Both surgeries were within a month of each other, neither was very long, and the recuperation process was not complicated. Jenna had worn hand braces before the operations, which she no longer had to wear after. The relief was instant! Thanks be to God, that neither surgery had been dangerous, and that both had been successful. Cooking, cleaning, and general household duties were much easier for her. And, not painful!

As soon as her hands were better, Jenna started job hunting in earnest. She answered an ad for a front desk clerk at a nearby motel, and went to give her application.

Before they hired her, she was hired as a bartender at a tavern that was right down the road from her Brother's house. She only worked there for a couple days, for several reasons. One, was that the motel hired her in the meantime, and she really wanted to be done with the whole bar scene. Two was they didn't give her enough hours to make the long drive worth it. So, Jenna began her new job at the motel. She learned all of the requirements quickly and enjoyed earning a living again. Jenna also got along with her other fellow employees and seemed to be liked by them.

During all of this activity, Jenna was getting things ready for the upcoming wedding. She had already chose the colors, decided that she would make silk flower arrangements rather than real, for expense purposes, and Steve's Aunt's and cousin's said that they would prepare the food. Once the menu was chosen, Jenna felt tremendous relief that that part was taken care of. Steve's friend, Billy, had a mother who sewed, and she agreed to help Jenna with wedding preparations. Jenna was going to have a dress made, rather than buy one. She knew she wanted a simple, off-white dress, with no frills. Steve and her had decided on black tuxes, with white shirts, purple vests and handkerchiefs. Steve wanted tails, and Jenna agreed. Things were really starting to happen.

The worst part of the house, was its proximity to the fire station. It was only one street over, and the siren was deafening. It wasn't long and they all grew used to it. Jenna had to admit, she enjoyed being able to walk two blocks for milk or cigarettes. That was often, as Steve smoked so much. They had a one car garage, that was old, also. It had a large empty space on the second floor.The only access to it, was to lift someone up through the hole in the ceiling. Jenna thought it would be a perfect space to store her patio furniture during the winter. One of her (female) best friends was a carpenter, and Jenna asked her if she would install a pull-down ladder in the hole. Of course, they had to afford the ladder first!

One other down fall, was that the plumbing in the downstairs bathroom did not work. The upstairs shower had problems also. Jenna had an old, neighborhood friend, who was a plumber. She called him, and he was very surprised to talk to her! They discussed the problem, the price, and the date. He spent the day fixing things, and of course, once again, Jenna paid him. There were two holes left in the wall and ceiling, that needed to be repaired when he was done. All it would have taken was one sheet of drywall, cut in half, nailed over the holes, taped, mudded, and sanded. Jenna had plans to paint the dining room afterwards. This was obviously too difficult for Steve, as it was never done.

There was also an enclosed, side porch, that was at the south side of the living room. It had windows all the way around it, and would have been a perfect mini-greenhouse. But, alas, it had an uneven floor. So, it was used for storage. The wooden staircase railing, was antique also. At the top of the landing post, was a place where a glass lantern used to sit. Jenna even had plans to replace this someday. The very first thing to be changed, was the carpet. It was brown, low-tweed, and in decent condition in most places, but poor in some. Jenna and Steve agreed on forest-green carpet, like the farmhouse had. The house needed painting, inside and out. Everything took money though. Money they didn't have. The house was bought in the summer,(with Jenna's $3,500.00 down payment, and good credit rating) and come spring, Jenna asked her six foot three husband to clean the gutters out. He was afraid of heights! Steve's younger brother came down to clean them. He was in his late twenties, still lived at home, rarely held a job long, and needed the money. And, family or not, they had to pay him!

WEDDING PREPARATIONS

Jenna originally wanted purple dresses. They already had black tuxes ordered, with purple and black print vests and handkerchiefs. The Girls and their Mom had looked in many stores, and could not find the dress they wanted. Two of Jenna's closest friends were to be the matron-of-honor and the bridesmaid. Nichole was to be the junior bridesmaid, and Charlise was to be the flower girl. Just by chance one day, they were in a small, family owned, local shop, when they ran across a black dress they liked. Since they all agreed on a simple dress, with no frills, one they could wear again, and at a decent price, maybe this black one would work! Nichole tried it on and really liked it. She looked good in it, too! Of course, she could wear burlap and look beautiful. Jenna asked the clerk if they had the receipt, could they return it, if her friends didn't like it. In the same shop, they then found an almost identical dress, in a smaller size, in purple. Charlise loved it! When Belinda and Grace saw the black dress of Nichole's, they really liked it, so, they went and picked theirs up that day. They brought them back to Jenna's house and they all chose a day to have them fitted at Billy's Mom's. Jenna was also going that day to have her dress discussed, and the material chosen. The clothes were pretty much taken care of, at this point.

Billy's Mom, Wanda, was also helping Jenna with the silk flower bouquets and boutonnières. After they discussed them, Wanda went shopping with Jenna one day, where they chose the bouquets holders, ribbon, silk flowers, and greenery needed to construct the arrangements. Fortunately, Jenna owned a glue gun, and so they began the job. It took a couple months to complete the task, but they did a nice job of it. The flowers were purple and white with subtle greenery. There were times that the task became frustrating. In fact, there were times Jenna could have tossed the things across the room, but she started it, she would finish it! That's the way she had been all her life, the way she had been raised. Never give up, keep trying.

One of the first things decided on, were the rings. The first place they looked, was a major department store that advertised its jewelry quite often. After Steve and Jenna had stood, waiting, at the counter for quite some time, and were treated like they were unimportant, they left, saying loudly, "You just lost a lot of money!" Next, they went to a smaller jeweler's, right down the row of a strip mall, and it only took Jenna a few minutes of looking, when she found the perfect ring! The engagement and wedding band hooked together, to form one, which Jenna thought symbolized their life together.

It was a little more than they had planned to pay, but Steve said to get them. He put a $100.00 down payment on them, and signed to make monthly payments. In the end, Jenna paid for them, too.

When they got out to the car, Jenna kept looking at her engagement ring and smiling. She told Steve, "You know, you never really asked me if I'd marry you, we just kind of decided to do it." Steve said, "Well, if you really need to hear it, Will you marry me, sweetheart?" Jenna replied, "Yes I will, honey." Jenna will always remember the day they told Steve's family. One of Steve's relative's even remarked how lucky he was to have gotten a cute one, with some money this time! One of Steve's favorite sayings was, "She (or you) didn't marry me for my money!" If she had only realized then that money was HIS biggest priority. Not his, hers! It was pretty much the same way with his family. The men depended on the woman's generosity. Her inheritances. That lesson was passed down to the younger generation. Jenna's family was just the opposite, old school. The man didn't really consider himself a "true" man if he couldn't support a wife and family. Jenna was always taught to help out with the finances, but that it was the responsibility of a man to support the household. Steve always thought that if he earned the paycheck, he could spend it as he wished! If he had cash in his pocket, he would spend it. Bills were to be thought of later, when he got around to it. Jenna had always paid her bills first. Even if she had to work three jobs to manage it! She finally had to put her foot down. They opened a joint checking,(Jenna kept a singular savings) Jenna told Steve's boss to please direct deposit his check to their account, and she made sure the bills were paid on time. Jenna made sure that Steve got his weekly stipend of cash for his cigarettes and what not. More than she ever got for herself! There were even comments made by members of his family, how it really wasn't fair for Steve to have to be financially responsible for her daughters. First and foremost, he NEVER was! Jenna received child support for one girl, that he sure didn't mind spending! And, if you marry someone with custody of their children, and commit yourself to being a step-parent, you accept both the perks and the downfalls of parenthood. At least, that's what mature folk do.

From the very beginning of living together, Steve had begun a close relationship with the Girls. He had even told them to call him Dad, if they chose. They called his parents, Grandma and Grandpa too. Both of Jenna's daughters needed good, family stability, with proper adult influence. Jenna thought she had that with Steve and his family. They have since damaged their family retrospect.

Jenna and Steve's mom planned and made the table centerpieces, and made some decorations to hang from the reception hall ceiling. Suns, moons, and stars, spray painted gold. They also planned the guest list and Steve and Jenna chose the invitations. Jenna addressed her sides and Steve's mom did theirs. They all discussed liquor choices and decided on them. A DJ was hired, and the cake was shopped for and ordered. Steve's friend's son was chosen to be the ring-bearer, and he was fitted for his tux also. Steve had picked his best friend's Shawn and Tad to be Best Man and Groomsman, his brother Daniel and his nephew Joshua to be ushers, along with Jenna's brother Jim. Both fathers were also wearing tuxes.

During these preparations, Jenna's Mother was getting sicker and sicker. The circulation in her legs had always been bad, but now it was almost non-existent in one leg. She eventually had to be hospitalized and have her leg amputated. One of the happiest times of Jenna's life was turning into one of the most painful. Her Mom still tried to be a part of the preparations, but she was never the same after her amputation. Jenna's Mom passed away, exactly one month before the wedding, and one day before Charlise's eighth birthday. It was hard for all of them to go on with the plans, but Jenna knew that her Mom would not want them to put it off on her account.

MISTAKE NUMBER THREE

The wedding was to be held on Sweetest Day. How ironic. So, on a clear, and beautiful day in October, the deed was done. Jenna rushed around that morning, getting things organized. Jenna, Nichole, and Charlise went up to a local salon to get "pretty" for the wedding. Jenna took some of the silk flowers to be put in their hair after it was done-up. Jenna had also made a ring of flowers, with long, matching ribbons that hung down the back, for Charlise's hair. Jenna had her nails done while Nichole and Charlise had a hair wash and got ready for their do's. Jenna's hair, which was half way down her back, had her hair put-up, with ringlets by her ears, and flowers placed in and around the up-do. Nichole also had her hair put-up, with some silk babies breath in it. Charlise's hair was done in ringlets, with the ring of flowers put on top. Jenna also had her eyebrows waxed and her make-up done. They all turned out very nicely. Steve told them how good they all looked, when they returned to the house. Jenna had even helped Steve with appearance preparations the night before. She had cleaned and trimmed his fingernails, given him a facial, and shaved the back of his neck. Steve hated to put lotion on, but the Girl's made him let them give him a back rub with some and put some on his dry, calloused hands. All the time, Jenna was trying to calm the butterflies in her stomach. She was wondering, even at the last moments, whether she was doing the right thing. Another sign.

They all rode to the church together, with their wedding duds hanging in the back. Jenna and the Girls joined the rest of the female wedding party, and Steve joined the guys. Jenna and the rest got dressed, and that's when she panicked! Charlise's dress was a little too loose, and the seamstress knew this and said she would alter it. She hadn't and now Jenna had to figure out what to do. Belinda had a safety pin in her purse, and Jenna pulled the material together in the back and pinned it. Everyone said that it was barely noticeable, so Jenna had to just leave it be. She also reassured Charlise that it was fine, now. All of the Girl's gave Jenna a big hug and kiss, and wished her the best, before the ceremony.

The only real decoration they had placed in the sanctuary, was a framed picture of Jenna's Mom and Dad, that sat on the alter table. Jenna and her daughter's wished she was here in person, but knew she was in spirit. Last night at rehearsal, Jenna's Father had broken-up when he had answered the Minister's question of who offered Jenna's hand to Steve. It was difficult for all of them to hear him say, "Her Mother and I do."

They had told the Minister to make it simple and quick, and Jenna also asked that the obey part be omitted. When they had repeated their vows, exchanged rings, and were pronounced Husband and Wife, Steve bent her over and planted one on her, that lasted a while! Jenna had considered that to be the most meaningful kiss of her life. At the time.

Some of the wedding pictures had been taken, outside, before the ceremony, and some during. The outside ones were taken behind the church, in the yard, under a big, old, oak tree, and they turned out great! A cousin of Steve's took the pictures, as a wedding gift. None of the pictures taken inside the church turned out. Yet, another sign.

There had been small bubble containers, tied with purple ribbon, made to give the guests in lieu of rice. Jenna had them put into a large, wicker basket with a handle, and Steve's niece handed them out. When Steve and Jenna walked out of the church, everyone clapped, whistled, and blew bubbles at the couple. Jenna's Dad had a blue, mini-van with two, rear, bench seats at this time, so the entire wedding party rode to the reception in it. Jenna's nephew, Sean, had decorated it with balloons and streamers, and wrote Just Married on the back windows, with shoe polish. The ride to the hall was fun, beeping the horn all the way. Steve whispered in Jenna's ear, "I love you, Mrs. Elliott. Other than when the Minister pronounced them Mr. and Mrs., it was the first time Jenna had heard this. She turned and gave him a big, wet kiss. She was so happy!

When they arrived at the hall, it was packed with guests, who were anxiously awaiting the Newlyweds. Everyone stood and cheered the couple, who both had huge grins on their faces. Jenna had asked the Girls if they were as happy as she was, in the van, and they both replied that they were. Both her and Steve had given them heart-felt hugs and kisses, as soon as the ceremony was over. When they all entered the hall, the first place Jenna stopped , was to see the cake. It was four tiered, with white frosting and fresh purple and white flowers on their tops. On the first tier, the top layer, was a crystal wedding topper, with bridal figurines. Just then, Steve's mother Louise walked up and joined Jenna at the cake table. She asked Jenna, "So, what do you think?" Jenna said, "She did a really nice job. The flowers make it lovely!" Steve walked up and joined them. "We should probably go to our table, hon, and get ready to eat. The natives are getting restless!" They went and sat at the bridal table, quickly shaking hands, hugging people, and waving, on the way. The champagne was already flowing, and Charlise said her tummy was growling. Jenna had purchased matching goblets and glasses for the wedding party, of dark blue with gold, suns, moons, and stars etched on them. She had also bought a couple of bottles of non-alcoholic, sparkling, grape juice, for all of the minors in the wedding party. As the best man poured Charlise a glass, Jenna told her, "We will be getting in a line to get our plates, in just a minute, Babe. And we will all be at the start.' Charlise leaned down and gave a kiss on the cheek and told her, "I love you, Mom. I love Steve too." "We love you too, Mouse."

The remainder of the reception was a success. The food was good and plentiful, the DJ played requested music, the bar had good reviews, the dancing was energetic, the gift table was overflowing, and the cake was delicious. When it came to cutting the cake, the cut was made without a hitch, and then it was time to feed each other a bite. As they approached each others mouths, with the cake in hand, Jenna's paranoia, (or maybe it was warning of things to come!) as they fed each other the cake, Jenna proceeded to smash the cake into his mouth. She smashed it with such force, that it even went up his nose! Everyone laughed, and Jenna apologized between suppressed laughter. Steve had to go to the men's room to blow cake from his nose, and wipe his face clean. Jenna met him at the doorway on his way out, to kiss him and tell him how sorry she was. Now, after all that had happened, she was glad she had done it.

SETTLING IN

Well, the deed was done. They both had to work the following Monday, as they were both fairly new at their jobs. So, between work and the Girl's school, things got into pretty much the same routine,as before the wedding. Steve worked third shift and Jenna worked first, so Steve usually got the girls off to school while Jenna showered and got ready for work. Both girls had medicine to take in the morning, check on homework, and make sure they were dressed for the weather. Charlise originally had to walk two and half blocks to the bus stop, but Jenna had written a note to the bus driver and the school board,(with a Doctor's note included) explaining how, with her heart condition, walking that far in inclement weather was indusive of future ill health. Within the week, the bus picked her up at the end of their street, which was one house away. Charlise's health improved immediately! Both girls attended different schools as their ages differed. Nichole went to the middle school and Charlise was in elementary. Shortly before Charlise's bus stop was changed, she had gone through a serious illness. She had complained of a sore throat for a few days, and Jenna had treated it as a typical, winter related sore throat. As days passed, the throat got sorer and a fever started. Whenever Charlise ran a fever, her heart started to race, because of the tachicardia. Charlise ran a fever of 99* the night before, so Jenna had already told her to stay in bed the next morning. Jenna had the day off work, so she intended to clean house, do laundry, and do some grocery shopping. And of course, take care of her Baby. Steve came home from work, and him and Nichole had breakfast together. Steve went on to bed and Nichole, school. While Jenna was cleaning up the breakfast dishes, Charlise slowly weaved her way down the stairs. She went to wrap her arms around her Mom, and began crying. It was hard for her to get any sound out as her throat was so sore. Jenna could feel the heat coming from her little body. She laid her on the couch, covered her with the afghan, and ran for the thermometer. 102*!! She put a cool cloth on her forehead and gave her a popsicle to ease the soreness. She took her to the emergency room and let Steve sleep. She wanted someone home in case Nichole needed them, anyhow. By the time they reached the ER, her heart was pounding! She was having her do the exercises her cardiologist had taught her, to lower her heart rate, on the way to the hospital. She was taught to put pressure, and grunt, like you would to have a bowl movement. This was pretty much a last hopeful gesture as they both knew how sick she was. Jenna carried her in and they saw her right away, as it was obvious how sick she was. By time she arrived her temperature was up to 104*, and her heart was beating a mile a minute! Jenna immediately informed them of her heart condition and that she was in line for open heart surgery soon. They did some swab tests on her throat and put a rush on the lab results. The ER doctor soon came in and told Jenna that it was Strep, and that they were going to transfer Charlise, via ambulance, to a bigger, better equipped hospital. Jenna agreed that this was a good idea, and laid her cheek on Charlise's hot cheek, and said, "Try to just keep still and rest, Baby. They will fix you right up, after a quick trip to another hospital. Mommy will be right back, I'm going to go call your Daddy and Steve." She told the nurse that she was going out to the pay phone, to please let her know the minute anything had happened. The nurse told her that she was welcome to use the desk phone, as long as it wasn't long distance. Jenna told her that one of them was, that she would just charge it to her home number. Don agreed to meet them at the hospital, and Steve told her to call should anything change or happen. They both agreed that he should stay there for Nichole.

In the ambulance, on the way, they were pulled over by a State Highway Patrol!! Jenna was freaking out! The officer came up to the window, and exclaimed that he was concerned, as they were going at a high rate of speed and did not have their lights on. The ambulance driver said that, "Yes, he should have had his emergency lights on, but that he had a very ill child in the back that he needed to get to the hospital! At this, the cop said to turn his lights on and be on his way. While in an ambulance, on an emergency trip to a hospital, to be stopped for speeding! Only this could be Jenna's luck!

Jenna's nerves and Charlise's health both survived this incident.

That spring, Jenna and Steve bought Jenna's brother's used computer; since he had bought a new one. They used wedding money. It was bought for the Girls use, but Steve must have thought it was his only, as he eventually had a friend tear it up for parts. Granted, it was an older model, but it wasn't his decision to make independently. Jenna's brother, Jim, also had a female dog- named Sheba, who was part wolf, part German-Shepherd, that due to have pups soon. Steve really wanted a dog. They discussed it at length, and since they had a fenced-in back yard, and the Girls had agreed to take care of one, they told her brother that they would take one, if they had first pick. Sheba had four pups, three were females, one was male. As soon as they were weaned, Steve and Jenna went to make their choice and bring him home. Yes, him. They chose the only male and named him Sable. He was almost all black, had kind, sad eyes, and fit right in with the family. Him and their cat, Jett, had a few run-ins, with fur and claws flying, but they were soon calmed down by someone! They also used wedding money to have Sable fixed, and both pets had their shots.

While Jenna was at work and the Girls were at school, Steve slept. That was his nighttime. Jenna woke him up every evening around six, to eat dinner with the family. She thought this was a vital part of a successful family life. This is when they not only shared a meal, but news of their day, their lives. Steve always told Jenna what a good cook she was, and she always tried to prepare and present a good meal. Nichole and Charlise took turns doing dishes, and they all helped cleaning up. If all of the Girl's homework was finished, they all watched TV or a video after dinner. They usually all curled up together on the couch. Jett and sometimes Sable joined them. (At separate ends of the couch!) They looked like the perfect family. Look closer.

A FRIEND IN NEED, IS
A FRIEND INDEED

Steve's friend Billy was now living in the neighboring state, with his Mother. He called them often, and Jenna could tell by his voice how miserable he was, and how much he missed his kids. She finally talked him into moving back, Steve got him a job, and they agreed that he could live with them until he got on his feet. Nichole was not thrilled with the situation, as she had to share her bedroom with him. He also worked third shift, so the sleeping arrangement worked out fine. She just didn't appreciate sharing her space! What teenager would? Sometimes Jenna's generosity overlooked her own children's happiness. Billy did try to help out with some of the housework, and Jenna realized that she could be a pain about it at times. Nichole remembers the saying well, "If you have time to drink it, you have time to throw it away!" They all liked soft drinks and the empty cans were a point of contention between her and Steve. Later on, Jenna mentioned to Steve's mom about how he shouldn't drink so much sugar soda, as his teeth were already bad. Low, and behold! It wasn't a week and Steve started to drink diet soda. But, according to him, he never discussed things with his mother! (In all the years Jenna had known him, she had never once, seen him brush his teeth. Now, it makes her nauseous.)

While Billy was living with them, there was a period of a few days when he didn't show up at home. Jenna tried not to worry too much, he was a grown man and a free agent. She finally called his Mom. He had a breakdown of sorts and was in the stress unit of the local hospital. Jenna told Steve, then called the hospital inquiring about visiting hours. She brought him some magazines to read, and a pack of cigarettes. They went to see him as soon as they were able. When they were preparing to leave, they overheard a couple of nurse's talking about Billy, and they weren't very quiet about it! About how this guy was freaking out, punching people and screaming. Jenna was immediately incensed! She knew that patients were not to be discussed, anywhere, at anytime. Especially not out in the public walkways, where they could be heard by anyone! Steve tried to calm her done, as he knew how much things like this pissed her off. On the way out, Jenna informed the registration desk attendant what had occurred, and how much it had upset her, and how she thought these two nurses should definitely be reprimanded! Jenna now feels the whole incident is so ironic, as she, herself has been a patient (prisoner) here.

When Billy returned home, Jenna and him had a long talk about what was bugging him. Billy, Jenna, and Nichole were sitting in the living room when he was telling them how he sometimes felt. He was saying how at times he was so depressed he couldn't cope, and he really couldn't pin it on anything! He just knew how awful he felt, how hopeless, useless, empty. But, then on other days, things were just the opposite. He felt almost high. Lots of energy, his mind racing with ideas, his mouth trying to keep up explaining them. Even spending too much money, as at the time, there was no end to it!

Jenna and Nichole just looked at each other, as if to say, "Sound familiar?" Jenna just hung her head and began to nod. Billy got quiet. "What, Jenna? Tell me!" Jenna walked over to him, laid her hand on his shoulder, and said, "I have a book I want you to read, Billy. It's about manic-depressive illness, and a famous woman who has it, how she found out, the problems it's caused in her life, and how she has dealt with it. It's a disease, Billy. It doesn't mean you're nuts!" Nichole told him, "I have it too, Billy. That's why I take Depakote every morning. It helps stabilize my moods." Billy just shook his head, as if he wanted this to disappear. He agreed to read the book, and thanked them both for being concerned. Later that same evening, Billy gestured to Jenna, and pointed at the front porch. Jenna smiled, knowing Steve had just left for work and the Girls were in bed. They sat on the porch and Billy pulled a nice, fat one out of his pocket. Jenna didn't smoke much pot anymore, but she often did with him. Billy leaned over and hugged her. "What was that for?", Jenna asked. "Well, I'm not too far in the book yet, but man, it's like reading about myself!", Billy exclaimed. Jenna took a big toke and nodded. "So, what does it mean if I am manic-depressive?", Billy wanted to know. After Jenna handed him the joint and exhaled, she said, "Take your pills every day, and get therapy. We all need someone to talk to, Billy!", Jenna replied, trying not to laugh. What they were talking about wasn't funny, it was the weed!

Billy was eventually diagnosed as having manic-depressive illness, known as bi-polar disorder nowadays. Jenna would never wish this disease on anyone, but she was very glad to be able to have assisted him in getting diagnosed and properly medicated. Helping others was second nature to Jenna, she COULD not stand by and idly watch someone suffer! Too bad others didn't feel the same inclination. Jenna also feels that anyone with a disability that is able to hold a job, or a position that enables them to help others, that they should do it! Self-esteem is a great source of healing, whether it be physical, mental, or both! Self-esteem, self-confidence, laughter, and God. These work better than ANY Doctor can.

That summer was busy and happy. Jenna and Steve held a small party on the 13th of June, to celebrate the day that they met. There were just a handful of close friends, lots of laughter, and swilling of brewski's. Before the party guests arrived, Jenna and Steve walked up to the new Steak joint in town. That sat at the bar while they waited for a table, and enjoyed small talk with the bartender. He had been a guest at their reception, and was telling them how much fun he had had. Anyone who saw them together could tell they were newlyweds, that they were still very much in love. Love IS blind, and so were most witnessing this union.

Jenna, with the Girl's help, held a garage sale that summer. It was mostly clothes that had become too small, and extra knic-knacs and such from around the house, and toys that had been grown out of. Tagging it was the real hassle, as Nichole thought everything should cost a fortune! They didn't end-up making a fortune, but Jenna got most closets, drawers, and toy boxes cleaned out! Jenna and Steve told the Girls they could have the garage sale profits for spending money on their vacation that summer. They could only take a day trip that year, as they were still both under a years hire at their jobs. Both girl's invited a friend, they took both cars, and went to a lake, with a great beach, swimming and camping facilities, on the border line with a neighboring state. They took a cooler full of soft drinks, sandwiches, and snacks for all, which they took turns helping to carry, two at a time, down a very, steep path, that led to the beach. They all thoroughly enjoyed themselves. Steve and Jenna talked about it, and decided to side track through Amish country on the way home, as they wanted to see it, and they wanted to show the girls, "how the other half lived." It was very interesting, and the Girls made comments about there not being any power lines to the houses. "How could anyone live without TV, or washing machines, or telephones?", Charlise asked. Jenna discovered years later that a lot of them actually had these "luxuries", they just hid the fact with generators. Had to keep up the image! Kind of like their marriage.

MARKED FOR LIFE

Early that fall, shortly after Jenna's Mom's death anniversary and Charlise's birthday, Steve had planned a tattoo party to celebrate Jenna's 36th birthday.

She had wanted one for a long time, and, hey, if they had a tattoo artist come to the house, had a party, where others might hire other tattoos ,there would be no charge for Jenna's! So, Jenna figured, all she had to do for her own birthday, was clean and prepare the house for a party, buy the party snacks and drinks, and get a FREE needle stuck in her leg ! Once again, Steve was home free. Jenna had now been at her job a year, so she took Thursday through Sunday off. That Thursday morning she cleaned the house well, mopping and shining floors, and scrubbing carpets. She made sure that the guest bathroom downstairs was ultra-clean, and even cleaned Nichole's bedroom, as they would be going through it to reach the bathroom. She then showered and got ready for her paternal Uncle's funeral visitation. Jenna was dreading this, but she respected her Father, Aunt, and cousins enough to attend. All she really felt like doing, was getting smashed. Jenna had never really dealt with her Mother's death well, and now had the stress of this party going ok. And, as much as she wanted it, she was nervous about getting the tattoo.

Jenna wore a black, pin striped suit with a black, satin blouse. She didn't want to look severe, just dignified. Steve was up by time she left, and he said that he would look after the Girls and fix them some spaghetti. Jenna hadn't asked them to go, as they really didn't know her Uncle. Jenna drove their second vehicle, which was a large Oldsmobile they had purchased from her Father. Steve was to meet her at a local tavern later that evening to have a birthday drink with her. She made her goodbye round of kisses and hugs and left. There was a bar right next to the Funeral Home, in fact, Jenna had briefly worked there at one of the times she had worked three jobs. She walked over and ordered a quick beer to ready her nerves for the scene to come. When she had finished it, she walked back over to the Funeral Parlor. Jenna made her obligatory visit to the casket, and then visited with relatives. After a short while, she joined some of the other guests who smoked in the smoking parlor. During a nervous cigarette, her cousin Ryan wished her a Happy Birthday. She wanted to invite him to her tattoo party, but didn't as his Father's funeral was the next day. They had always gotten along well, even though they didn't see each other often. Jenna went back into the main room and stood talking to her Dad's oldest brother and his wife for a few minutes. She then got ready to leave. Jenna said her, "I'm sorry's", and passed out hugs.

Jenna left the Funeral Home and went West to her hometown. She stopped at the Tavern there, that she had frequented for years. This is where she was to meet her love, her Husband. Jenna sat at the bar, where she usually sat, and ordered a beer, the usual drink of her choice. She visited with the regulars, and Kathy , the bartender. While she waited for Steve's arrival, she called two of her friends to see if they would come up for a birthday drink. Jenna realized this was a long shot, as they were coming the next night to her tattoo party. These conversations are bleary, and not totally remembered, word-for-word. Two different parties have reported two different conclusions to these conversations, but as Jenna remembers, neither of them said they could make it. Unless someone actually overheard these conversations, or were a part of them, they are not able to say exactly what was said. That's just common sense.

When Steve arrived, he got a beer also, and the two of them talked about where to celebrate their first anniversary, with the owner and his wife. After staying a little while, Steve had to leave for work.

Jenna Slone

The Girl's were home asleep, with no sitter. Jenna switched vehicles with Steve, as she liked the Blazer better. Steve denies knowing that Jenna had been drinking, even though he drank a beer with her. She wasn't drunk-YET-but she felt no pain. When Steve left, Jenna had another beer. This is when certain people asked if she wanted a ride home, because they could tell she had a buzz. Jenna was foolish enough to turn them down. At this point, Kathy suggested that she take her home as soon as the bar closed, and that way Jenna could stay and get all fucked-up! Jenna agreed and GAVE Kathy her keys! There was a woman who was a regular there, who Jenna knew fairly well, and her birthday was the same as Jenna's. They proceeded to do shots of Tequila together. Then, Delores had to leave. While sitting there alone, waiting for Kathy, Jenna's impatience got the better of her good senses. And her bull-headed stubbornness. While Kathy had her back turned, Jenna snuck behind the bar and took her keys back! No one took her fucking key's!! She made the fucking payments!! All of that drunken bravado and STUPIDNESS. Jenna left.

'TIL DEATH US DO PART?

Jenna took the back roads home. She knew she was drunk. The rest of this description, of the actual accident, is from what Jenna has read and what she has been told. She has no memory of this. Jenna always wore her seat belt, she didn't think one could tell your kids to wear one, if the parent or driver did not. Whenever Jenna would get in the car, she would automatically put her belt on and lock the doors. Old fears never die. And, start the car, light a cigarette. Habit. The Blazer had a much better radio than the Olds did, that's why she traded vehicles with Steve that night. So, I'm sure she had the tunes cranked as she made her drunken way home. Jenna knows this for sure because this information was written in the official police report. Approximately a mile before the accident occurred, a Police Officer passed her, saw her swerve, knew she was obviously impaired and a danger to other drivers, but since it was ONE mile out of his jurisdiction, he did not turn around to pull her over. To her knowledge, he didn't even call it in! Before this incident, Jenna would have been glad for this job indifference. Now, she sure wishes that he had done his job! I'm sure there is at least one other family that wishes the same thing! From his written statement, it was not long after passing her that he heard the crash. It was then that he turned around to see what had happened. What's that old saying, "A day late, and a dollar short!" What really happened here, is only really known by three. Jenna, the Male Driver, and

God. Jenna has absolutely no memory of this, and as she is now on Medicaid, they will not cover the expense of hypnosis, which would answer a lot of questions. Unfortunately, the Male Driver has taken this information to his grave, and unless Billy Graham or someone has a direct line to The Almighty, that's his secret. It happened on the corner of a country road that intersected a busy State Route that ran North to South. Jenna had traveled these same roads thousands of times before, and knew them well. She had always loved to drive, and had driven all over the country. She had even driven in Canada and Mexico. Jenna had a fairly clean driving record, as of late, that is. She had been stopped for two DWI's in the early 80's, so she did know better about drinking and driving! Yes, it had been years since she had even had a speeding ticket, so, like most drivers, she had grown pretty smug about her driving skills.

There have been conflicting stories on how the accident actually happened. Some have said that Jenna ran the stop sign and pulled out in front of The Male Driver. Others have told her that she did stop, and then proceeded to pull out in front of The Male Driver. It was still Jenna's fault, as she caused the accident, stop sign or not, and she was legally intoxicated. When she pulled out in front of said Male Driver (or drove), he did not even have time to brake. There were no skid marks on the road. He hit Jenna in the passenger side door, broad-siding the vehicle. He was killed instantly. Part of me is glad he did not suffer, mostly I am sick that I caused this. There has not been a SECOND that has gone by since, that I haven't wished to trade places with him.

From witness statements on the condition of the vehicles, and some pictures that were taken of Jenna's vehicle, the right, or passenger side was hit with great force, the left (or driver's side) was practically untouched. She was also told that he must have been traveling at a high rate of speed, as after being hit in the passenger door, Jenna's car spun all the way around, leaving an imprint of her rear spare tire (that was attached near her back windows) in his driver's door. Jenna has also heard different tales on whether she flipped the vehicle or not. In the pictures she has of her car, there is grass and weeds stuck in crevices all over the vehicle. It's really all irrelevant, as it doesn't change what happened. Jenna's NEVER drinking and driving, is the only thing that could have.

Jenna's Driver's License was still in her former married name (Don's last name). Story of her life! Once they ran the plates, they knew who had co-signed on the car, and that was Steve's father. They called him and told him of the accident. Steve was called at work. Steve's Aunt, who lived next door to his parents, went down to their house and woke and told the Girls. Jenna's Dad was told, and he informed the rest of the family. They all headed to the largest trauma hospital, across the nearby big city, where the emergency Life Flight helicopters flew to. This had been Jenna's ride. When they found Jenna, she was legally dead, herself. No heartbeat, no respirations, no discernable pulse. She was first seen by the nearest town's Paramedics, who then called for Life Flight. Jenna is not really sure which ones revived her. There have been MANY days that she wished they hadn't. Jenna thinks she knows now why God saved her, she will always think that she didn't deserve it. "I'm sorry", just ISN'T enough.

IN SICKNESS, AND IN HEALTH ?

Steve and Jenna had only been married 11 months, 6 days when the accident happened. Their marriage truly ended that morning. Yes, Jenna had drove drunk, and had known better than to do it. She had NEVER meant to hurt anyone, let alone her own family! The accident itself was just that, no matter what ANYONE said. An accident. Jenna never meant to run a stop sign, pull out in front of anyone, or certainly not kill anyone! And, you know, this was not her way of getting attention, taking time off, or testing anyone's love and devotion. Although, it was a good test in the end.

After the ER had examined Jenna and determined the extent of her injuries, they rushed her to surgery. She had a 10 centimeter gash on her right forehead, deep enough to see her skull and her brain, which was swelling. Both eyes had been knocked for a loop, the right eye being the worst. There was also a fairly deep cut on her face, directly under the bottom lip. They think this may have been caused by her teeth. Luckily she had worn her seatbelt, but it left deep, dark bruises across her breasts, chest, and stomach. In fact, it had caused her bladder to rupture. Well, the impact had caused the seatbelt to hold Jenna in her seat and keep her from being ejected, but had caused the rupture in the process. Her right leg was pretty smashed up, also. Both top (femur) and bottom (tibia) were broken, the femur being the worst. It was broken in two places, the tibia was only fractured. They inserted a metal rod with big screws in Jenna's femur, to hold the leg in place, and make (what was left of the bone!) grow straight. It went from hip to knee. Jenna could now tell you what the weather was going to do better than the local news, just by the feeling in her right knee or butt cheek! Jenna had numerous cuts, mostly from all of the broken glass, and several smaller broken bones. Some had been set, some had not. I guess when you are busy trying to save someone's life, a pinky isn't all that important!

They shaved Jenna's head around the gash in her forehead, and placed a pressure gage in her skull to measure brain swelling. It never swelled enough to require brain surgery, but it came close on a few occasions. There are 4 levels of coma, level 4 being the deepest. At this point, Jenna was a level 4. Jenna was comatose for seven months, most of this time in a stage 3 coma. Jenna was placed on all sorts of life giving machines, for breathing, monitoring heartbeats, measuring oxygen levels, and eventually a feeding tube, catheter, and fecal bag. A tracheotomy had been placed in her neck early on, to open a blood-free airway. When they had put this in, they were in such a hurry to start an airway, that one of Jenna's vocal chords were damaged. She has an impaired voice to this day. But, like the finger, they were in a hurry!

She has also just learned that her sinuses were all but crushed, which has led to much breathing difficulties.

After surgery, Jenna was put into an Intensive Care room. Close family members were only allowed in for ten minutes each hour. This is how Nichole and Charlise saw their Mom. In ICU, with all of these tubes running in and out of her body, with the sounds of machines whirring and thumping. If this wasn't devastating enough for the Girls, less than 24 hours after the accident, in her ICU room, over her lifeless, tube and machine ridden body, thinking they were watching their Mother die, a CRUEL statement was made. Nichole and Charlise, and Steve and his mom were in the room, everyone visibly upset. Right in front of the Girls, obviously within their hearing distance, Steve's mother said to him, "Maybe you should think about divorce. It looks bleak, what does she expect you to do now, take care of HER girl's?" Well, that's what marriage and being a step-parent are all about, aren't they?! "They could go back to their real father's now." In other words, let you off the hook! Jenna had thought she had had Mother In Laws from Hell before, but this was just Evil! Divorce-now?! If he had half a brain, he'd wait until I croaked and the house and all the bills would be paid off!! Unfortunately for him-I lived. But, he enjoyed spending child-support in the meantime!

Charlise did end up going back to living with Don. It was made easy for him when no one put up a real fight. What? Pay for a lawyer to keep her here, when you didn't want to take care of her in the first place?! It's hard to admit, but, Jenna is now glad that Don and his wife did take care of her all this time. She had a comfortable, safe place to sleep, three squares, and people who TRUTHFULLY cared. All of this makes Jenna grateful Steve is sterile. And it breaks her heart that her own family never offered any assistance to the Girls after the accident. How convenient to think (or hope) everything was being taken care of by the husband and the in-laws! As long as Steve said that things were fine, they left it alone.

Jenna remained in critical condition for about a month, where she stayed in the ICU. Nichole has told of how she almost always had her eyes open, even while comatose. How very creepy for the Girls! Knowing now that all of those crocodile tears shed by Steve and his family, were just a show. Jenna had felt like such a FOOL when she found out- but NO ONE makes a fool out of her!!! NO ONE.

FOR BETTER OR
FOR WORSE ?

Someone on Steve's side of the family decided that since either Belinda or Grace was supposed to meet Jenna at the bar that night, it was almost their fault that she got plastered and had the accident! Even IF they did stand her up-which they did NOT-that is so ridiculous!! Jenna is a grown woman, able to make her own decisions and be held responsible for them. Her parents raised her to be honest-take blame where it is deserved. Never automatically find fault with friends , they weren't holding a gun to her head!! Because of this further wife's tale, Louise informed the nurse's that Grace, nor Belinda were allowed in to see Jenna. Jenna's two best friends! Who was she to decide? They both were very upset about this. Grace would have liked to kick her pompous ass, but knew that the family was under enough stress. Whenever Louise wasn't there, they told the TRUE circumstances to the nurse's and were able to see her. Jenna's Father spoke for them on their behalf. He was a mess through out all of this. After losing his wife of 47 years only a year before this, he didn't know if he could take this loss, too.

Quite a few people came to the hospital to see Jenna, while she was critical. It was good to be seen crying and carrying-on, making sure people were aware of your family ties and past alliance with Jenna. It was all exciting right then. Everyone thought she would die.

Jenna knows there are some who are disappointed that she didn't! One could pretty much compare visiting Jenna in the ICU to going to a Funeral visitation. Make sure you,youself looked decent, you never know who might see you! And just like making the obligatory coffin pass, they would be let in to see Jenna in small groups. After clucking your tongue in order to suppress tears, hugs and best wishes were passed around. The only difference here was –no "I'm sorry's." Some of those concerned people have not been see by Jenna or any family member, for that matter, since! What really makes Jenna literally nauseous about that whole show is-Jenna really didn't need their personal assistance anyhow-she was unconscious!! But, her husband and her children needed them!! Her Father, for that matter! Help with housework, or even their school work. Who in the hell could concentrate? Or some good, old, emotional support. LOVE.

As soon as Jenna was taken off life support, and was off of the critical list, she was moved from the hospital to a nursing home. Once it has been determined that a hospital can't do anymore for a patient, they get shipped off to a nursing home. If a hospital has done what they can, and you are still too sick to go home, a person gets "stored" with the old folks.Even if you aren't in need of total nursing care any longer, but your "family" doesn't have the room, time, or care to take care of you, this is where you stay. It offers the constant nursing care one might need, but as far as personal, hands-on, love, or devotion, forget it. They can't pay people to give a shit! This way, visitors could come for a short, temporary visit, feel better about themselves for taking the time out of their busy schedule, and the patient could attest to the fact that they did show up!

Jenna (still in the coma) was moved to a local nursing home with a dubious reputation for good, clean care. But, hey, it was closer to her husband and his family than the hospital was, and since their convenience was much more important than Jenna's outcome, that was all that really mattered. Different people have told Jenna since, that it always smelled like urine there, and that a female friend was asked personal questions about Jenna's menstruation. When she asked why was she being asked instead of a family member, they told her that they never came to ask! So having Jenna moved sounded like a good idea, at least it made them sound good, but they were much too busy to be bothered with a smelly, depressing nursing home! Jenna was comatose anyhow, she didn't know the difference!

Nichole tells her Mom now, that she bugged Steve until he took her. Coma or not, she needed her Mom. Nichole was trying to get through High School then, and it had been rough going. Nichole did end up graduating, and Jenna is SO, very proud!! With little to no help from any so-called family members. Plus, Nichole kept a job also. Had to. She liked to eat. Nichole would often come to see her Mom with her guitar in tow. She has a beautiful singing voice that her Mother loved to hear. Nichole would play and sing to her Mom for hours. Jenna knows that that Angel's voice helped bring her back.

Charlise wasn't with Nichole and her Step-Dad for very long after the accident. Don wanted to make sure she was being taken care of, and there was the revenge factor, also! Now that Jenna knows the truth behind her own husband's motives, she is grateful for Don's taking care of her Baby too! At least she had decent meals and a roof over her head! The change of custody was very difficult for both Charlise and Nichole to understand and get used to. They both should have had some intense counseling, and a lot of comforting hugs. Too bad most people involved, were too selfish thinking of their own problems. Jenna can say better than most, "What comes around, goes around." In Jenna's humble opinion, there are some things in life that are almost impossible to forgive, and child-abuse or molestation are definitely two of them. There are other ways to abuse a child. They don't have to be beaten or full of bruises to be damaged. If a child hears, sees, or experiences horrible things, at the hand of an adult, what kind of role model do they have for their future life? Jenna just hopes and prays that she taught them not to believe all that they hear or see, that their own intuition is much more reliable than some fools words or deeds.

Jenna was a patient here for a short time, when she contracted pneumonia. She was then transferred to the large teaching hospital in the nearest big city. In, of all places, the rehabilitation department! I'm not sure what they thought they could rehabilitate when Jenna was still deep in her coma! I hear that they did do range of motion exercises while she was there recovering from pneumonia. That was to keep her muscles from atrophying. Jenna has learned quite a few medical words since waking up. She is so very thankful that the intelligence part of her brain was not damaged also, as she most often is alone at doctor's visits, and had to decipher their directions herself. Of course, when the doctor's know that they're alone, think they are too damaged to understand them correctly, or since they are on Medicaid, the doctor's not being paid enough to take the time to explain their injuries in detail. Everything in life is ALL about money.

When Jenna had recuperated from the pneumonia, she was transferred again to another, larger, nursing home. This was in the late winter of the same year as her accident. Jenna was put in a private room, but was moved again because the roof (ceiling) in the room began to leak when the snow began to melt. Right before they moved her, Jenna began to have some almost conscious moments. This is when (that she can remember) Jenna had several visions, or vivid dreams. This is one of them: Charlise was there to visit her with her nephew, Sean and her sister-in-law Janice. Janice was talking to her, while Charlise and Sean goofed around with each other. Janice was telling her how close the two of them had become lately, and Jenna remembers feeling almost jealous! Yes, she could hear and understand just fine. For some reason,(don't ask me why-coma dreams were not her specialty!) they went outside to say Goodbye. When Jenna went to hug Charlise, she pulled away. Charlise was angry at her Mom, because Jenna thinks Charlise thought Jenna was acting like she was unconscious, that she really wasn't! Jenna cried and cried (on the inside), as she wanted to wake-up so desperately! She could hear things around her, was aware of some of her surroundings, but was still on the frustrating threshold between being comatose and awake. All she wanted was to put her arms around her Girls and hold them tight! Jenna had no memory of what had happened, or why she was there, but she knew she missed her Babies.

Another one of Jenna's visions or dreams was of her physical therapist, Bob. The only reason for this that Jenna can think of, is that she saw him 5 days a week. Bob gave her range of motion exercises every weekday, to keep her comatose muscles from stiffening up. Jenna must have known she was moving to a new room, as this is what the "dream" was about. For some reason, Jenna knew that Bob was married. She thought she was going home with Steve that day, and that a few of his friends were helping him take her, Billy included. Bob's wife's clothing was hanging in her closet, in her new room, and even though she couldn't talk yet, she was trying to tell Steve what she wanted to wear home. Jenna didn't have any, really, spiffy outfits to put on, and so she was going to "borrow" one of Bob's wife's for the weekend. Jenna remembers that it was a pair of black slacks, a gold shell, and a black, and gold jacket. Steve and his friends did come for a visit that day, and Steve knew that she wanted to come home. Because of this "vision", Jenna thought that she was leaving that day. When Steve held her, (as best he could!) and explained to her that he couldn't bring her home yet, as she was still too sick, Jenna cried and cried. Her heart felt broken. This wouldn't be the last time she felt this way over the next few years!

AWAKE FROM THE DEAD

Jenna does not recall when it was that she woke up exactly. Which room she was in, or who was even with her then! She does know that, even though things were fuzzy, she knew who she was, who her family was, and pretty much, what was happening around her. It was extremely frustrating not being able to speak! She could hear and understand all that was being said around her, and could not respond! Jenna could only answer questions by a nod or shake of the head.Jenna felt no pain at this time, just fear and confusion. One of the worst moments in this time period, was Jenna's first shower. Now that Jenna is more knowledgeable about such things, she does know that she was in a Jerry-Chair at the time. She wasn't strong enough to even hold her head up yet! It took at least three nurse's aids to give her the shower. Jenna was terrified! She still didn't know: why she was here —what had happened-why she couldn't talk-who these girl's were-why she was all fucked-up! She does remember that the shower water felt good, but her skin was very sensitive to the water temperature and the washing of her skin. She was unable to help, as her right arm and hand were useless at the time. Jenna does remember that she was unco-operative and a down right pain-in-the-ass, and she apologizes to those girls now! They do not get paid near enough for what they do! They do a nurse's job, and get a quarter of the pay! After the shower, they stuck her in the Jerry-Chair and put her in the nearest TV room. This would have been fine if Jenna had a pair of glasses! Jenna had worn them since the fourth grade, and hers were broken in the accident. It sounded interesting! She couldn't even yell to tell them at the nurse's desk, across the hall. So, she sat, and dozed, until they came and got her. Jenna was not a happy camper, between the shower and the "closet" storage.

During this time, Jenna had many visitors. The news had gone out! Jenna was awake! She saw people that she hadn't seen in years! Jenna is now so thankful that some relatives who have since passed-on, came to see her. In fact, she probably misses them most now, as they never passed judgment on her, but always loved her unconditionally. One of those misses the most, was a sister of her Mother's, who she loved to chat on the phone with. There had been so many times that she almost picked up the phone to call her. How she wished that she could. This is when Jenna still could not talk. She could not verbally communicate with them, or even hug them as she wished, but through face movements, limited body language, and LEFT hand holding, she expressed all the love she was possible of.

One of Jenna's dearest friends came to see her with another male, close friend, whom Jenna had not seen in a long time. Jenna was embarrassed to be seen in such a place, but glad to see them all the same. While Melissa was there, she noticed that Jenna spent most of her time in the bed, and had no TV to watch. Jenna did have a stereo that someone had placed in her room, while still in her coma, that had a note taped to it, that said, "Please keep on channels 92.5 or 104.7". Those were the main "rock-n-roll" stations in the nearby area. Jenna was a middle-aged-hippie at heart. Steve and anyone who knew her well knew how Jenna loved her classic rock and roll. Melissa brought her a small, colored TV set, that Jenna had to keep set on a certain channel, as it had no remote and Jenna was unable to lean-up and change channels yet. Jenna did not want to press the call light button and bother the nurse's aids to change the channel! They had too much to do as it was! Jenna only wishes Melissa knew how much that TV meant to her. It filled many, lonely hours. Why is it, no one in her own "family" saw that she needed a TV? Were they truly coming to provide Jenna with the love and certain personal

87

needs she may want, or did they come for show? After all, one had to prove they were loyal to a family member in need, whether there really were or not.

The staff members at this particular nursing home were fantastic to Jenna! Sure, there are a few rotten apples in every bunch, but most of them truly cared for this girl (woman) not much older than they were. There was one girl in particular that Jenna felt close to; Stacy. They often laughed like idiots together, not discussing illness, pain, or bad stuff. In fact, it was usually sex, men, or partying together when she got better.Jenna felt almost "normal" when talking to Stacy, even it was only intellectually. They had a lot in common, they found. They both liked beer.This was before Jenna knew why she was really there, that beer had done her in! She had no memory of that night, and no one told her squat!

Another staff member who helped her out tremendously, was a member of the activities staff.All of the activities staff was good to her, and her recovery, providing exercise classes Jenna attended every week-day, Bingo and Bunko games that Jenna often won (that gave her "mad money".) and a group called the Lunch Bunch that went out to a restaurant once a month, and could even order a drink if they chose! Those people are certainly old enough to decide, and lonely enough to deserve it! I remember that soon after this occasion, a bill was sent to my husband, and him and his parents got snippy with me about a strawberry margarita I had ordered. First of all, it just sounded good, I couldn't even drink the damned thing yet, as I choked on most things, and the glass was too damned heavy for me. So, sorry they had to pay for a drink wasted. Back to the activity staff. Juanita, knew how badly I wanted to speak. Her other job was with mentally disabled young people, and she had had some experience with people who could not speak, such as Autistic youth. Juanita would bring a tape-recorder in my room and help me with my speaking lessons. It took just a few sessions to be understood! Boy, the first recordings sounded funny! It was so good to be understood. It was still somewhat garbled, so those who understood translated to those who didn't. This was a MAJOR step to independence.

Jenna still had a feeding tube in her upper torso. Jenna hated it. The nurse's often threatened her to fill it, as they knew how she hated that, and she wasn't gaining enough weight to please them! (Oh, to have that problem now.) If it was filled too quickly, it would make her throw up. As she couldn't sit-up and vomit away from herself, she often puked on herself. Oh, joy.She was thinner then than she had been before the accident. That made her happy. As soon as Steve and the Doctor agreed, Jenna went home for a weekend, Mother's Day. There had NEVER been a more excited and happy Jenna, one full of anticipation and hope. Steve's parents brought dinner over, and ate it with them. Jenna was still hard to understand, but everyone made do. It was SO good to be home! The only thing missing was Charlise. In a way, she was glad she couldn't go upstairs, that way she couldn't see Charlise's bedroom. Steve and Jenna slept in Nichole's bed that night. Steve gave her medicines through her feeding tube, helped her dress, and Louise even came and helped change her diaper! It was wonderful to sleep with her husband that night. They made love as best they could. It didn't take much more than a passionate look to make Jenna orgasm!

Nichole has told her Mother now that during all the time that she was comatose and in hospitals and nursing homes, NO ONE ever came to help with household duties. But,if they heard that laundry wasn't being done or the house was messy, that it was Nichole's fault. Jenna had even been told this. Nichole was expected to keep house, go to school, work, do the laundry, and make sure there was something around to eat! Now, Jenna realizes she was mostly to blame for this, but, what about Steve's family, that didn't want their precious, baby, boy to suffer any hardships? And Jenna's family, Nichole's Aunt's, cousin's, or Jenna's friends? Later, Jenna even found out that Steve never bought garbage bag tags, he just put the bags of garbage in the garage, over top of the lawn-mower, bug-zapper, and garden tools. Eventually, it was all garbage.

Jenna made rapid improvements at Swan Park. Her Father took her for glasses, and that helped tremendously. Her right arm grew stronger and increased in movement every day. Her voice also steadily got better.Jenna thinks her swift improvements were because of two aspects: (1.) The loving care of the staff at Swan Park. (2) The trips home, to her own house, her own things, and her own family. (And, the sex was a bonus!) When Jenna was at home, she wanted to get up, help Nichole and Steve with the laundry, cooking, and housework! Not that it was bad when she was there. She just wanted to feel useful again. Steve and Jenna went shopping one day, and bought potting soil, seeds, and plants to put in Jenna's two flower boxes kept on the porch. He knew how Jenna loved gardening. It was good therapy to have her hands in the dirt! She knows that he really DID care then.

The Elliott's had an above ground swimming pool, given to them by Louise's Mother.(So was the property and the house.) They all helped get Jenna in the pool a few times that summer, and into the floating lounge chair, to sunbathe. A lot of the time, Steve would just stand by Jenna's chair, gaze into her eyes, and tell her how much he loved her. If he only knew, (or cared) how much that meant to her.Nichole had a couple of choir concerts at school that Steve took Jenna to that year, also. Sitting in the audience, next to a friend and old neighbor of their's, listening to her beautiful daughter's voice was Heaven to Jenna. She had never asked for much, and this was Nirvana.Jenna and Steve went to Nichole's High School Graduation that spring, followed by a Graduation Party at his parent's house. Proud can not describe how she felt that day! Jenna still can not understand how Steve and his folks could care then and not now. Or was it all just an act?

Towards the end of her stay at Swan Park, Steve walked into the dining room, where she was eating lunch. Jenna had other company that day. Her paternal Aunt and Uncle, along with her cousin Rhonda. They were partial witnesses to this happening. Steve pulled a ring box out of his pocket, and Jenna instantly knew what it was. In the accident, the hospital had cut the wedding rings from her swollen fingers. Steve had them repaired and cleaned. They looked beautiful to Jenna! She had missed them so much! Her family quickly said their goodbyes and gave them privacy. Steve wheeled her back to her room, got down on one knee, opened the box, and with a tear in his eye, asked her to marry him again.(Jenna's roommate was asleep, usually was.At the age of 100 though, she could get around a Hell of a lot better than Jenna could!) Jenna had no memory of their first Anniversary, so they planned to re-new their vows on their second. Jenna was busy during these months, getting ready for the ceremony and also to move to another nursing home, closer to her house and her family.

Everyone at the Home congratulated Jenna, and proceeded to throw her a Going Away Party, the following week. They had a cake, and decorations, and gave her a necklace that says, "Someone Special." Jenna wears it often and will always keep it.

She knew she would miss the friends she had made here, but was excited to be making the last move, before going home.

FOOLED BY A FOOL

The whole time Jenna languished in these luxurious accommodations, she fantasized about going "home" all the time. All of her nurse's aids were probably sick of hearing about it. Steve and her had discussed, at length, about them trading bedrooms with Nichole, what with the stairs and the bathroom being right there. Nichole was fine with having the master bedroom! Jenna would have been able to walk up the stairs with minimal assistance, twice a week to shower. That would have even been good exercise for her. She also planned on doing as much cooking and housework as she could. She would have help from nurse's aids who were to come twice a day. Nichole was thrilled to be off the hook! Jenna thought these were the plans anyhow.

It was decided to re-new their vows at the Christian church uptown. They both wanted it simple;nothing elaborate. They just wished to express their love and complete devotion to each other, their marriage. They even wrote their own vows! They still wanted the Pastor to say the original vows of a "Typical" marriage, but wanted to add their own declarations of love. During this whole time, Jenna was so happy, and full of love, she barely even thought of her own predicament. Steve's mother and Aunt took Jenna to a Mall, to shop for a wedding dress and a gift for Steve. Jenna shopped at a store she knew had reasonable prices, as she didn't want to seem greedy. She found a really cute black, with a light gold print, short, chiffon dress. It had spaghetti straps and a small, matching jacket. Jenna already had plenty of black pumps to choose from, and since she wouldn't be walking in this ceremony anyhow, she mostly had to make sure they fit her still, slightly swollen feet. Jenna found black, satin pajama shorts, and matching, short robe for Steve. I guess since she didn't actually pay cash for them herself, they weren't really considered a gift from her heart, to his. His new woman probably loves sliding her hands over the satin now!

Jenna was nervous. Not about re-marrying Steve! She loved him SO much, and planned on staying married to him forever. And she thought he felt the same way. She was nervous about her impaired voice. As far as being in the chair, everyone who was invited knew, and she had never gave a hoot what others thought anyhow! Her opinion had always been that if they didn't like what they saw, don't fucking look. In saying her own vows though, she wanted to be understood. For everyone there to know how very much she loved Steve, how grateful she was to him for sticking by her, and how she always wanted to be Mrs. Elliott. The day was sunny, and brisk. A perfect Fall day. The small chapel filled up quickly, as it wasn't often one saw a "freak" wedding! Jenna didn't feel this way about herself then, she actually felt pretty today! With everything that has happened since, her self-confidence has suffered.

The ceremony was beautiful. Jenna even carried her original silk-flower bouquet from their first ceremony. Jenna does not remember their own vows, word-for-word, but she remembers this part. Jenna compared the love she felt for Steve to some of the love stories and partners she had seen in the movies. Like Rose's love for Jack in Titanic, Marrin's love for William in Braveheart, and Aarwyn for Aragon in Lord of the Rings. Everyone said she was understood perfectly, and that her vows were succinct. Steve's vows were great, I'm sure, but Jenna was so enwrapped in them, that she doesn't recall them now. One wonderful, make your hair on the back of your neck stand up moment, was at the end of Steve's vows, he took Jenna's face in his hands, looked her deep in the eyes, and said, "I will ALWAYS love you, NO matter what, Jenna. I will NEVER leave you." At that very moment, the stained glass window behind their heads, their profile's, shone as a beam of sunlight streamed through, encircling them in it's light.

When Jenna was still in her coma, at the very last of it, Steve applied for Power-of-Attorney. He knew Jenna was expecting a nice-sized check from Workmen's Comp. for the carpal tunnel she had suffered. Steve did not actually receive the Power-of-Attorney or the check, until Jenna was awake and coherent. Jenna had enough of her memory to remember the money owed to her, and was able to somehow sign the check, and disperse the funds. But, alas, no mention of the check was made to her or Nichole, who was doing her best to help keep things afloat. The check was for $5000.00, $1600.00 of which went to Jenna's Workman's Comp. Lawyer, the other $3300.00 was hers. HIS. Jenna realizes that her income was no longer contributing to the family budget, and she would have gladly helped out in any way that she could, but was never given that chance. House payments could have been made in advance, utilities paid-up, the savings padded. Why pay bills when you need to pretend you are flush and impress friends and prospective lays? Why be a responsible adult when your own parents are telling you that because of your intense grief, you are owed a good time!

After the re-newel ceremony, there was an informal reception dinner held at a local nice restaurant. Only about 10 people were there, but Jenna could have cared less! She was SO happy! And so much in love. Jenna was COMPLETELY in the dark about so much! People thought they were protecting her by not telling her things that THEY deemed upsetting. It upset her much more to have to find out details from professionals involved in the case. Especially from Steve. Before the first ceremony, Jenna had sat Steve down and said, "I have learned the hard way, that being honest about things, especially feelings, no matter what, is so important to a marriage!" Steve agreed, and they both decided that they did not want to proceed without promising each other to always be honest. It all seemed so sincere. One never knows what catastrophry leads to. That is one piece of advice Jenna has for prospective brides or grooms. Ask them-straight out-"What would you do, how would you handle things, if I was incapacitated for some length of time, or permanently? What if you found out, that it was of my own doing, my own fault? Would you still love me, still go by the wedding vows? Steve was excited about the prospect of suing someone, the bar, the other driver's family, someone. Rumors were flying at this time. It was all so confusing to someone who was so clueless as to what had even happened! When Jenna and Steve re-newed their vows, the question of whom they might, or could sue, was still up in the air. No wonder why he wanted to still be her husband?! This followed his entire families plot. The man did as little as possible, and the woman provided the job, the inheritance, and the prospects for financial security.

That night, Steve had got them a suite at the motel where Jenna worked. Once again, if Steve had used his fairly, intelligent mind, he would have asked them for an employee discount when registering. But, when you know it all, you need no assistance.

Steve had a beautiful, crystal vase, full of a dozen red roses, waiting for Jenna in the motel room. (She probably paid for them with her Workman's Comp. Money!) They also shared a glass of wine, from a bottle gave to them by Juanita, Jenna's vocal coach from Swan Park, who came to the ceremony today. The love they made that night was as intense as ever, with some tears shed by both of them. Louise even came to help get Jenna dressed the next morning, for her return to the nursing prison. How could she have been so fooled by people who claimed to love her so unconditionally?!

MORE TIME SERVED

That Fall, Jenna moved to another nursing home. Nursing Home #3. This one was in her and Steve's home town, and only a couple of miles from the house. It was called Fulton Place, and was right next to the local hospital. Jenna and Steve had tried to find a home that was known for it's good rehabilitation department. This was difficult to do as all homes had therapy, but almost none had young residents. If you were 75 and had a stroke, they could help you. If you were 38 and had a bad accident, Good Luck. Since this home was next-door to a hospital, people had told them that their therapy department was sufficient. Jenna's therapist and friend had even told her that this was a good place to recuperate. So, she went. It was easier than Jenna had anticipated. Steve's father and younger brother took her in their van. The nurse's aids at Swan Park had helped Jenna pack her paltry belongings before she moved. The bummer was: she had to leave the wheelchair that she had grown accustomed to. It had to stay at Swan Park. She had to leave with no chair. If they would have had to stop anywhere, Jenna could not leave the van. Once they arrived at Fulton Place, they provided her with a chair. Of course, it was too tall for her, so, they had to replace it with a shorter chair. Story of her life!

The rooms were better here, in the fact that they were single rooms, with a shared bathroom between. They were very small, but what can you expect for only $4000.00 to $7000.00 a month ? Otherwise, it was pretty much the same ordeal. Same bland food, same young, inexperienced, and uncaring helpers, adequate activities, if you were 90, with the loneliness being even greater. Steve and parents visited quite often for about the first two months. That was the whole reason why she moved, wasn't it? One of the best days Jenna had here, was one day Nichole and current boyfriend got in a big fight, and Nichole came and cried on her Mom's shoulder. She wasn't happy that they were fighting or that her daughter was upset, just that Nichole needed her Mom, and that Jenna got to comfort her, best as she could.

Jenna did go to therapy most days, but after they evaluated her and determined that she couldn't do much, Jenna could hear in their voices that they didn't hold much hope. That made her feel the same. As soon as Jenna reached a place where she was pretty much at a stand-still, as far as progress, she was delegated to a group of nurse's aids, called Restorative Aids.Physical Therapy would not let Jenna stay at a certain "plateau" long enough to let her body get used to it, before she moved on to the next challenge. Some of these new exercises were things her body hadn't done in years! It was fine in the long run, as Jenna made good friends with almost all of the Restorative staff. Standing was becoming easier, even though she still had to hang on to something, on the sides. She knew this was a matter of balance, something she really didn't understand. And Doctor's had never really explained to her. Oh well, it was only her life!

Jenna didn't have a recliner, to sit in comfort in her room, so her Dad went and bought her a new recliner! Jenna thinks it was because he felt useless as far as knowing how to "fix" her, so this was a way to help. He came to see her, at least twice a week, bringing his Chihuahua with him. This is when the famous Mexican restaurant's commercials were popular, his name was "Paco". As soon as him and Jenna's Father came through the doors, Paco wanted down, as he knew the way to Jenna's room. Even when Jenna moved to different rooms several times, during the course of her stay, Paco would go with Jim once, then know his way. Every time her "Pops" came, it was special, but there was one time that was extra special. That was the time he brought Charlise for a visit! Don and his family came up from Florida to see to the former house in Ohio,(Jenna's old house) and to go to his Father's funeral. Even though he had all of this to deal with, he made sure Charlise saw her Mom. She only stayed for two days, but she saw her Mom twice, and spent time with Nichole and Steve , and even spent the night at Steve's parents house, as Steve no longer lived at "home", he was just waiting for the bank to take it.

Holidays were spent with Steve and his parents at their house this year. Things were pleasant with Jenna not knowing the real truth about things. They probably found this amusing, even laughing behind her back at every opportunity. Yes, Jenna was grateful to escape from her "Hell Home", but she was fooled into believing they all loved and cared for her. Steve even took Jenna shopping for Christmas presents for the Girls and a friends kids. Of course, Jenna paid. Louise helped wrap the gifts, as Jenna was unable at this time. Jenna's Dad took one of the big gifts with him, in his car, to Charlise, as he was going to shop for a place down there. Everyone was still extremely cordial to one another, with some of us being in the dark, and all!

Jenna had dropped out of High School, November of her senior year. She even had a fairly good GPA! She was already engaged to Nichole's Father, he was in Louisiana with the Military, she missed him terribly and all she needed was an excuse to quit! An argument with her teacher solved that problem. Therefore, Jenna had been considering getting a GED since waking up. Might as well do something with all this time on her hands! An agency that helped disabled people , helped Jenna get some GED study material, Jenna studied, took the test, (which her Father went with her) and passed! Afterwards, it was determined that it could only be considered a practice test, as Jenna did not have a valid driver's license or Ohio ID. She still felt like she had really accomplished something, and was more determined than ever to get the "Real" GED!

The same helping agency had helped Jenna apply for her Social Security. It was determined that she could get quite a large chunk of change, which was back pay, money she should have been receiving for at least a year, but no one had been inclined to do so. Jenna lost out on about a cool grand, because of some one's procrastination. Jenna bought an electric scooter from a local Medical Store. It cost a pretty penny, but Jenna had to shop by phone, with no assistance. Jenna has learned that whenever "professionals" know a person is disabled, they will take advantage. This electric scooter enabled Jenna to go out to the smoking gazebo to smoke. Yes, she had started smoking again. And the nurse's at the home said it would be impossible for her to get assistance opening the doors to get her scooter out, as the aids were always so busy. Jenna knew it was because they just didn't want her to smoke! People think because she has brain damage that she is thick as a fucking book! Or bright as a cave. So, Jenna just rode up to the door and pushed it open with the scooter, and off she went! Tell her no, will ya? Jenna tried to make the time go by. She had way too much time to think. And worry. And feel sorry for herself. Word did reach her, the grapevine grew here too. Part of normalcy is jealousy. Part of jealousy is love. Sick as that sounds. As time went by, visits came less and less.

Some of the "roommates" Jenna had, made things more difficult. They were all ancient, some were loud, others paranoid, some were just nuts.Jenna knows that she could be a royal, pain-in-the-ass at times. Finding out you're handicapped, living with dinosaurs, and you're whole family is messing with your head, is enough to make anyone that way! One thing, or person that helped with all this was an aid, named Lee.

TEMPORARY FRIEND

Jenna had never been a shy person, and she was very grateful for this fact, since she had met so many "strange" people and been in so many weird circumstances during these tumultuous years. One of the women that Jenna met soon after moving into Fulton Place, was an aid named Lee, who always worked second shift. They hit it off immediately. They often laughed at some of the other employees and residents. Neither of them were cruel people, they both had had some tough spots in their lives, and knew that having a sense of humor was vital to survival. They found they had much in common. They were almost the exact age, only separated by a few months. They both had an oldest daughter of the same age and grade in school. The main difference was that Lee was lucky enough to have stayed with the same husband for quite a few years. It wasn't long and Jenna got to meet Lee's family, husband Oscar and four children. One girl and three boys. It also wasn't long before Jenna grew to love this entire family. She spent many good times with them over the years, sharing Birthday Parties, Holidays, and summer bar-b-ques. And, quite a few beers. Jenna appreciated the fact that they made her feel normal, liked. For her, not for who she used to be. They had never known her before. Jenna bought them all Christmas presents that year, not for anything in return, it just felt good to have true friends. They even took her camping once, and that was a fun experience!

That summer, Lee took her to an appointment Jenna had with one of her former lawyers. Jenna's father had taken her that spring, to find out who's fault the accident actually was. Before she spoke with him that day, she did not know much about the whole incident. After finding out the truth, her entire life changed. The first thing she did when she found out, was bawl her eyes out, and the guilt of it all, almost did her in.She was glad she was with her Dad. Part of her wanted to ask him, "Why didn't you tell me?" She realized how distant their communication had been all her life, though. Steve was expected to visit that evening, at the home. Jenna was seated in her recliner, as usual. Steve came in and gave her a kiss hello. He asked her how it went that day. He knew she had seen her lawyer that day. Jenna had always been open, and honest with him. Jenna started to cry, softly. She responded, "He told me that I was drunk, ran the stop sign, killed the man, that it was all my own fault." Jenna went to hold him, and he put his hand on her shoulder, and pushed her away. "I can't deal with this right now!", he exclaimed, as he turned and stomped from the room. Jenna was doubly devestated.After that day, he ignored her for a month. No visits, no phone calls, didn't take or return her calls, nothing. This started a trend of ignoring her. When he did start seeing her again, is when the whole subject of divorce came up. That was also the instant their intimacy disappeared from their marriage. It seemed every time Jenna saw Steve for the next couple of months, all he talked about was divorce. But, Jenna knew what a procrastinator he was, and that if anything was going to happen, she had to do it. Jenna wanted to put the signal out, "Put up, or shut up."He seemed surprised when he got the papers. This whole time, Jenna was developing a close friendship with Lee and her family. One that she thought would last a lifetime. One where the disability didn't matter, that their relationship was based on friendship, not ability. But, like her marriage, this was another dream , never to come true. The second time Jenna saw this lawyer, Lee took her to see about filing for divorce. She knew that because of her fault in the accident, she would stand a better chance if she initiated the divorce, leveling her own barrage of charges. Jenna was also interested in asking him if it was possible to sue the bar she had been at that night. She did not yet know the details of that night, she only knew that they obviously had served too much alcohol to her and that she was not cut-off soon enough before she drove. Jenna really wanted to be told by someone separate from the whole incident, who was impartial to the outcome. She knew he was a true professional, with only business on his mind. He had told Jenna that day, that there was a good chance of suing, that he would look into it and let her know. After filing for divorce that day, Jenna felt so empty, so hopeless. Lee helped restore her calm, her sense of self-worth. Lee had a way of doing that for her, with seemingly no problem.

Lee and Jenna spent a lot of time together that summer, sharing lots of laughter and sisterly hugs. Both Lee and Steve knew about the chance of suing the bar and both had dollar signs in their eyes. Lee and her husband Oscar began talking to Jenna about moving in with them, taking the downstairs bedroom that was next to a bathroom. They knew how badly Jenna wanted to get out of the nursing home. So did all of Jenna's family, but did anyone offer her a place with them? Hell no. Way too much hassle. Jenna told Lee and Oscar, that even if she couldn't sue, she could give them at least $400.00 a month for rent and living expenses. She even discussed moving in with them with her caseworker at the home. Jenna pretty much thought it was a fait accouplie. Until she found out that the statute of limitations was up, she could no longer sue. Yet, another thing no one had helped her with, or looked into. Oh, there were family members who said they were so pissed about the bar letting her drink so much, and let her drive, but not mad enough to get off they're butts and press any charges! During this time, Jenna went with Steve for an eye surgery. Once he found out there was a chance for moola, he became more attentive. He still treated her as if she was contagious, but the ignoring her temporarily stopped. On the way to the surgery, they talked at length about suing the bar, and even what she would do with all the money! They even decided on a more local lawyer to proceed with the case, as he was much less expensive, in case it didn't work out the way they wanted. Jenna appreciated him taking her, does to this day. Then, they talked about the divorce. Steve told her how surprised he was to get the papers. He also told her, that he thought that they should put it off, at least until the lawsuit was decided and the custody suit for Charlise had begun. Once again, Jenna had been fooled into believing there was hope for them, for the marriage. Too bad for Jenna that once Lee and Steve knew there would be no windfall, they were pretty much history.

Jenna withdrew her divorce file, and lost $400.00 in the process. In the meantime, Steve had agreed to seeing a marriage counselor. Jenna's psychologist said that she would be glad to talk to them. Jenna was happy to have someone outside, looking in. So, the appointment was all set-up, with Steve being mailed all of the times and dates. Two days before the appointment, Steve told Jenna, on the phone, that he was not going to tell their problems to a stranger! Jenna asked him why did he say that he wanted to go, then? Jenna knew it was a lost cause. Jenna went to the appointment. Steve never showed up. All of the intense love that Jenna felt for Steve was slowly turning to anger, distrust, and even hatred, at times. Jenna realized, that their problems originally started with the accident, but if they could move-on together, it could still be good. One more large part of her life-over. Time to move-on.

SAVED AGAIN

Jenna started dealing with an organization that helped disabled people, through the nursing home. She was finally starting to admit to herself that she was permanently handicapped, no miracle was waiting around the next corner, and that when in this condition, you had to rely on other's help , from time to time. Jenna had always regretted not graduating high school. She had been correct in the fact, that she did not need a diploma to be a wife or mother, but she wanted her children to be proud of her. And, be proud of herself. Especially now! And, since she had all this time on her hands, might as well use it constructively. Jenna inquired about getting her GED, received study material, and set-up a date and time to take a practice test. They made arrangements for her to bring an electric typewriter, as it was still difficult for her to write longhand. Jenna's Father took her, and carried the typewriter for her. Jenna passed with a fairly high score! But, low and behold-there was always a fly in the ointment for Jenna. After she had passed the practice test and was ready to set-up an appointment to take the "real" test, they informed her that she needed an Ohio picture ID, which she did not have. She was determined to get one, but knew it would be difficult, as relying on Steve's help was doubtful, and it sucked so bad not driving herself! (It took him a year-and-a-half to take her.)

Jenna's Nero-Surgeon talked her into having a Baclifen Pump put in her abdomen. It was a round, fist-sized container, that held a drug called Baclifen, that controlled leg spasms. The container was connected to the spinal column by a catheter, or tube, that would administer the Baclifen to her spinal column, and then to her brain, hence stopping the spasms. Up until that point, the spasms had been controlled by pills, but since she had been more physical lately, walking farther, and farther each day with the Restorative Aids, her spasms had increased. Therefore, it did not take that much cajoling to talk Jenna into the surgery, as she was willing to help others help her, in anyway possible. Everyone that Jenna knew, knew about the surgery. But, Jenna had told them the same thing that the Nero-Surgeon had told her. That, it was an OUTPATIENT surgery, home the same day, with little to no risk involved. Even though Jenna was never told that medical students would be involved in the actual surgery, she surmised that some would "observe", as it was a teaching hospital, with college right in the name. Jenna had learned through experience, that if you are alone,(which she most often was) and you are on Medicaid, details are limited, things are more briefly explained, as time is valuable, and your time does not pay as well.

Jenna went to surgery alone. No surprise. First-she was used to it, and it wasn't supposed to be a big deal! Next thing she knew, she was groggily waking up, with two young looking "doctors" standing over her. She started to feel very dizzy, light-headed. She heard a monitor go off. Jenna's blood pressure had dropped very low. She was alert enough to hear one boy say to the other, "What did you do? Cut her artery?!" Jenna must have passed out at this point, because everything fades to black here. When she did wake up again, she found out that she had almost bled to death, had been given four units of blood, and that her blood pressure had dropped dangerously low. They had in fact, cut an artery!

An outpatient, minor surgery, had turned into a life-threatening ordeal.Jenna ended up being in the hospital for four days. The only family member that came to see her was a paternal Aunt, that lived close to the hospital. I guess she didn't come close enough to death to warrant attention! She felt like a foolish, sick, hopeless, lonely, guinea pig. Jenna did not mind being used as a teaching implement, or being seen naked by strangers. She had been seen nude by so many strange people , up to that point, she should have been doing porno, at least she would have been making money!! The Nero-Surgeon and his staff, of course, denied that anyone had cut her artery, that it was because of something her own body had done.This was ONE thing, that was not Jenna's responsibility.

Soon after this,Steve told Jenna he had rented the house to a couple of friends,that the rental income would make the house payments.Now,neither "friend" had a frickin job, and he never made them sign a lease! These items of interest weren't known to Jenna,until it was too late!One of these,so called "friends",was Billy!He moved into the house,where he and his girlfriend,stayed in Steve and Jenna's bedroom.With Jenna's clothes and belonging's still in the dresser drawers,and in the walk-in closet.To this day,she's still missing a lot of her stuff.Of course,no one knows what happened to it! Billy now tells Jenna that the house was a pig-sty,that it was so bad,it should have been condemned!! Jenna had always been a neat freak. Even working full-time,she managed to keep a clean house. Steve had been out of work for a while, and to hear his family talk, they helped out SO much! Some of the neighbor's have said that the yard didn't fare much better. Jenna was embarresed,and she wasn't even there! Like I've said, Billy's girlfriend lived there with him. I can see Steve, licking his lips and rubbing his hands together, in anticipation of another "friendly" challenge! Steve had a nasty habit of messing around with friend's girlfriend's.Or wives.I guess he didn't think he could get someone decent on his own! He has caused all kinds of trouble by being so heartless,even having a gun pulled on him!Why his "friends" continued to forgive him,has always been a mystery to Jenna!Maybe it was a sympathy friendship.

Steve and Billy's girlfriend started to hang-out.They were seen together all over town.Steve and Jenna's dog,Sable,still stayed in the back yard,and eventually moved into Steve's parent's basement. I guess Misty grew to like Sable,and after he moved,she would use him as some cockle-maimy excuse to visit Steve at his parent's!So,it's rather obvious that mom and dad knew about Misty!But,hey,Jenna drove drunk,so those wedding vows didn't include her!Misty was a much bigger drunk than Jenna had ever been,but if you had never hurt anyone,including yourself,that was ok.

In the meantime,Jenna had heard through the grapevine that the house was soon to go back to the bank.Her heart was broken.Steve called that day and wanted her to go with him to sign some loan papers at his lawyers.Here,they weren't loan papers at all!Here,Steve had already borrowed six grand from a friend,(who had inherited it from his dead father)and was trying to buy time from the bank!What Steve wanted Jenna to sign,(unbeknownst to her)were papers stating that she owed his friend the money also!!That was all taken care of,by Jenna's no-nonsense attorney,later.What a Weasel!! To think she was married to this bum.Bum # 3.

When Jenna heard he was about to lose the house,she panicked!She had priceless and sentimental antiques at the house! And,piss on her stuff,what about Charlise's?! Nicole had already got an apartment with her boyfriend,(at 17),after paying most of the household expenses for a year,or more.So,she had already moved her belonging's out,and took what she wanted or felt she needed of her Mom's.A couple of Restorative aid's from the home,who she had become good friends with,took her to the house one afternoon,after Jenna had explained what was going on.She managed to get her antique china,that belonged to her Grandmother,some old books,and a few pictures.One of her friends let her store the stuff in her attic.She will be forever grateful for this.

Jenna was getting closer to "escaping" every day!She had been working closely with a woman from a local Ability Center,on getting her own apartment.She was SO excited!!To get out of here,was the answer to her prayers!She didn't care if she got a cardboard box,as long as wasn't here.It really wasn't a bad place,she was just much too young to be here. Two of the best memories Jenna had of this place, were getting her nails done every Friday, by the Activities staff, and the help, and friendship she got from the Restorative staff. She knew she had really gotten quite a ways, physically, they always told her how good she was doing. She sure was trying her best !

Jenna tried to decorate her room, as best she could. Her room at the other nursing home was dull. First of all, she shared it with a 100 year old woman, whom Jenna could not communicate with, and had NOTHING in common with ! Other than the stereo someone had had in her rooms since the coma, that Jenna still wasn't sure who brought it, and the small, portable TV that her close, friend Melissa had been kind enough to bring, NO ONE had seen fit to bring some life into her room! Considering since she spent most hours of a day in this room! Jenna's bed looked like a giant crib! It had high side rails, I guess so she wouldn't fall out. That's kind of funny, actually, as she was unable to roll on her side, and always slept on her back ! She did have a small side table, where she kept her typewriter, her only REAL means of communication. Jenna had a terrible case of hemorrhoids (husbands) then, what a pain-in-the-ass !! They were understanding, and kind enough to let her get off her butt, and back into bed by noon. She slept a lot also, as some of her medications made her sleepy, and her body had taken one hell of a beating !!

At Fulton Place, her Father brought her this really neat bird-house,on a short,post,and a plastic,flower pot that had dancing flowers. He also brought her a beautiful,porcelin Angel, with a flowing, white dress, and hands clasped in prayer.That was something she did a lot of! God probably got tired of her bugging him! "Oh, it's you, again!!" Sometimes Jenna spoke to her Mom, too. She often felt her arms, wrapping her up in one of her famous, hugs. Jenna begged them both to watch over both of her girl's, as she couldn't. They did.

CLASS OF 2001

Nichole was to graduate High School, this spring!! Jenna was SO PROUD. Steve's parents were having it at their house.No one else had offered. Even if it was just for show,Jenna was very, thankful to them. They wanted to celebrate it in their large, back, yard, but the weather didn't co-operate with their plans ! Jenna wanted to help out so badly, but was really, unable. That made her feel so useless. She wore a knee-length salmon colored dress, and looked half way decent. Louise served punch, coffee, and cake, and everyone seemed to have a nice time. Nichole received gifts and some cash, which Jenna now hopes, didn't pay some of Steve's bills!!

The Graduation ceremony at the High School was extra special for Jenna to watch. Mostly because ,this was her Baby, Graduating!! That through all of this, she had stayed in school, finished, and Graduated with her class !! Jenna had quit, November of her senior year, to marry Nichole's father. Young, and dumb.

Sitting right in front of Jenna, was a girl-woman she had gone to school with, and her kids. She was still pretty, and she had always had a bubbly, personality, and had a smile for everyone. She was popular, as her father was a big wig in the schools. Jenna had always liked her though, and would have liked to say, "Hello." But, she was embarrassed with her voice, so, she was quiet. Besides, this was Nichole's day!! When Nichole walked up and got her diploma, Jenna wanted to stand-up, clap, and holler,"Hooray!!" Of course she couldn't, so instead, she clapped as best she could and yelled as best as she could, "Alright Tink!!" That had been her nickname, for as long as Jenna could remember! At the end of the ceremony, when they threw their caps into the air, tears streamed down Jenna's face. She felt proud enough to burst !

Later, at the party, people came and went, as the day went-on. Nichole's paternal Grandmother came, with one of her father's sisters and her husband, a niece, and a close family friend Nichole had always called, Aunt Bonnie. Ever since Nichole was small, she had pronounced her name as, Finny Cole. So, that's what Aunt Bonnie had always called her."Finny Cole" was glad to see her. Jenna often wondered where all these loving people were when Nichole was struggling to keep it all together! Nichole's father never showed. No card, no call. He did buy her a gift, that Jenna and Nichole were forever grateful for. He was stationed in Las Vegas then, Nichole and her Grandmother had flown out there, and she had her senior pictures taken in Vegas. Nichole's Grandmother said that her father had paid for them, and,"Yippee!!"if he did, but her Grandmother probably spent the dough, and told everyone he did. Either way, Jenna was grateful, and they turned out great!! She had always been quite petite, like Jenna had been most of her life.BC. Before Children, Jenna had always claimed.Having two c-sections had a way of changing a body! Jenna wouldn't have given that scar up, for anything!!

Speaking of scars, Jenna was soon to have, yet another. Shortly after the graduation, she felt a rather large,lump, in her right breast. Now, she had Fibro-cystic breasts, "Lumpy Tits", she called them, so, when they swelled up once a month, they felt lumpy. But, this was different.Usually, she could move them around, and squish them a little. This was bigger than usual, stationary, and she couldn't "squish" it. It felt almost solid. It made her nervous. She told the nurse, at the home, but of course, they couldn't fart without getting a Doctor's note ! Jenna called her Doctor's office the next morning. They wanted her to come in that day, but the only transportation Jenna had, insisted on a weeks notice! That week of waiting and wondering were pure torture. While waiting for the appointment, Jenna had Steve feel it. He was even hesitant to touch her breast !! Jenna even told him,"If it is Cancer, it's not contagious!!" Sometimes, Jenna wished it was malignant. Not for attention. She knew better. How much closer to death could she get ? If this didn't capture their attention, why would breast cancer ?!

When her Doctor examined it, he looked concerned. That really made her nervous! He scheduled a mammogram. Jenna knew how much those hurt! She had always said,"Let me put the Doctor's nuts on that table, and let me squish 'em with that machine!" Whenever they had you in the process, they would ask,"Comfortable?" Jenna knew they had to ask this, she just thought it was an asinine question. Low and behold, they couldn't find the lump on the ex-ray. Then Jenna had a son-a-gram.There it was, in all it's glory! Jenna was then scheduled for a lumpectomy. Jenna was scared, and yet, resigned, at the same time.

Jenna was awake during the operation; they only used a local anesthetic. She asked the nurse, at the beginning of the surgery, if she could see the removed lump of tissue, afterwards. The nurse seemed surprised at this request. She said,"Are you sure?" Jenna replied,"I want to see what's causing all this fuss!" With the local, it didn't hurt, but Jenna could hear them cutting, and pulling it out. What a strange sensation! The Doctor said the operation was over, and they went to whisk her out of the room, when Jenna asked the nurse where the tissue was. It had already gone to the lab. "Sorry." So, Jenna asked what did it look like. The nurse responded,"Like bloody, chicken, fat." Yum.

Jenna had to wait another week for the results. She told her Dad,"If the cancer doesn't get'ya, the stress will kill 'ya!" When Jenna finally received the call, she answered with baited breath! They explained to her, that it was deep, tissue, bruising, from the seatbelt! Benign. She took a big, sigh, of relief! Jenna always wore her seatbelt. It had saved her from being ejected from the vehicle, but had caused her bladder to burst, and now, this lump. Yes, these things had been awful, but, Thank God, she didn't look like Frankenstein!!

Nichole told her Mom, how glad she was, that it wasn't cancer, that she wanted her to stick around, crippled or not !! Jenna wrapped her arms around Nichole, and said she was glad too, and told her once again, how proud she had been at the Graduation. Jenna had even, already decided, that if it was cancerous, she was not going on chemotherapy!! She had been through enough, and she didn't want to spend her remaining time, throwing up, and being sick!! Now, as she looks back, she has seen firsthand how valuable chemo can be. She's just thankful, she did not have to face that, too.

THANK GOD,
I'M FREE AT LAST !!

Jenna's caseworker from the local Ability Center, came to see her one day, and had great news. There was an apartment, in town, that was available, if she wanted it ! Jenna said that as long as she could afford it, and it was a two bedroom, she would take it ! (Who was she kidding?!She would have taken a cardboard box, if it meant getting out of here !!) The following day, she went to look at it, and sign some papers, with her caseworker. So, it wasn't handicapped accessible ! But, it was big enough for her furniture and belongings, and had a laundry room, (and since Laundromats were out of the question, having her own equipment would come in handy!) If she still had it !! It also had a one car garage. Not that she had a vehicle, but it was a place to store stuff. She had insisted on a two-bedroom, as she still had the fantasy of getting custody of Charlise back! She knew she would at least get some visitation.

They talked about what handicap equipment she would need in the apartment. They decided on what things were needed, Jenna and her went to the apartment Manager's office, signed some papers, Jenna shook their hands, and thanked them both, with a big, goofy grin on her face ! The apartment complex was called,"The Projects" by most people in the community. Most people were prejudiced enough to think that if you were poor, you were criminal, or substandard. Jenna is the first to admit, she used to feel the same way ! So, she had gone from owning her own house, and having respectable employment, to being on Government Aid, and living in low-income housing. She had realized a long time ago, that she had no where else to go, so, might as well make the best of it ! What's that old saying ? "When life hands you lemons, make lemonade."So, she would squeeze them suckers, do the best she could !!

The last two weeks at the home were a whirlwind for Jenna ! Of course, there were a ton of papers to fill-out and sign.Gotta kill those trees !! She made it a point to personally say goodbye to employees and residents she had been friendly with. She had one last meeting, with the owner, and at least one person from each staff that she dealt with. A few of them said a little something, about how she was a nice person, and knew how hard she tried, but that she could be a royal, pain-in-the –butt sometimes ! They all laughed! All but the owner, that is. He was not famous for his sense-of-humor!Then Jenna said her piece. How she was grateful for all the help she had received, realized she could be a pain at times, wished that there was a rehab home for younger people, that there should be at least one per state. That some of them had become dear friends, but, she would not miss them !! She had never been shy about expressing her feelings! That had always been a strong belief of hers. She would much rather be told THE TRUTH, about feelings, opinions, or happenings, than be made to guess ! She knew that some were holdings back on some subjects now, on count of her injuries. They figured that she had been hurt enough, she didn't need any more stress. Jenna just wished they realized, that it was more stress, not knowing the facts! But, she's tried to understand where they're coming from, too. It was a first time situation for all!

Jenna moved again, in the dead-of-winter. Some Aids at the home helped her pack what paltry belongings she had there, and she was ready to go. Her Father had also purchased a nice, forest-green recliner, for her room. It even had an electric vibration control in the seat! OOOH, she liked that!!But, that summer, she traded it for a lift chair, she had found in the paper.She had received her S.S. back pay, and it was at a reasonable price. She had priced them brand new!WOW! She wanted to sit in it, not fly it ! She had also bought an electric motor scooter, which she knew she had paid,WAY TOO MUCH for, but she needed it to get around. Steve borrowed his dad's truck, and came that evening to help her move. She had also had him bring her chaise lounge that summer, with its cushion, as she loved to lie out in the sun. He did.He had to buy a new cushion for it, as the old one had been left out in the weather, and was no good.Another form of procrastination. Jenna was just glad to have it here.Beings that she got so bored here, was tired of TV, couldn't do much, physically, she laid-out a lot that summer.Between laying-out, and Steve's parent's pool, she got nice and brown that summer.Jenna tanned fairly easy, anyhow! So did Charlise! Poor Nichole. She was fair skinned like her dad, and burned easily. She wasn't wild about the hot sun, anyhow!

Jenna was HOME now. They had put-up a safety bar, and provided her with a shower bench in the bathroom, and her hospital bed was in the bedroom.That's really all she needed, to get by on.Most of her stuff was just put in piles, unorganized, and basically a mess. Neat freak that she was, she didn't care for now, she was FREE !!

A few days after moving to her apartment, Steve brought a truck full of Jenna's furniture and boxes, that had been stored in a storage unit. When Jenna had learned that she was losing the house, she had Steve take her to their Realtor's office, where they also made arrangements, and took payment, for their storage units. Jenna had some money put away, so she paid for a year's storage, in advance. No way, was she going to lose her belongings too ! She'd already lost HER house ! Some of her furniture were antiques.Handed-down antiques, with much sentimental value. Items she planned on handing-down to her girls, and Grandchildren. Little did she know, that when Steve moved the stuff to the storage unit, he picked and chose what he wanted to keep! I am sure too, that his mother helped decide what to keep away from Jenna! Pretty much anything and everything that his parents, or anyone in the family had given them, they determined that those items were Steve's, not Jenna's.That's all right. Little by little, as time went by, Jenna pitched or gave away anything that was connected with this family. Wedding pictures, anything worn on that fateful day, cards, albums, knick-knacks, you name it, it was HISTORY! Pretty much, like they had tossed Jenna aside, like a used tissue!

Jenna's garage was full. Floor to ceiling, front to back. And her apartment was a literal mess. One of Jenna's nurse's aids recommended that she call a local volunteer organization, that would help disabled or elderly folks with minor tasks around the house. She called and asked for assistance, with this mess she had been left with. While she waited a few days for them to arrive, her brother and sister-in-law came over, bringing some items from her Father's house, her childhood Home. Some she had asked for, and some were a surprise. Her Mother had told her years ago, that there were some things she wanted Jenna to have. An antique sideboard w/mirror, that Jenna now used as her entertainment center, a wooden chair, from a one-room school house, that was very old,(Her Mom had always called it the "Captain's Chair".)and her Dad's micro-wave! Now, Jenna knew that was old too, it was the only micro-wave she could remember from their house! She sure appreciated this! One day, low and behold, Steve brought over a radio-alarm clock, and a new micro-wave oven!! Jenna told him how grateful she was, but her Dad was giving her his, it worked fine, and if he really wanted to buy something, she could use a VCR for all her movies. He took the micro-wave back, and brought her a VCR.

In the meantime, that volunteer organization had sent a husband and wife over to help Jenna with this jumbled disaster! Wow!! What a difference! They came every Thursday, for a few weeks, (it took that long!) They put together bunkbeds, hung wall hangings, moved furniture around, and even hung curtains. It actually was starting to look like a real Home, now! It had been a very, long time since Jenna had been surrounded by her own belongings! Having her Mothers and Grandmother's things around her, comforted her also. Jenna proceeded to fix-up the spare bedroom as Charlise's room. It had HER bed, HER pink dresser, (that Jenna had hand painted, with white hearts on the pink, front) wall hangings that had been on her bedroom walls at the house, Jenna even filled the drawers and closet with Charlise's clothes that she had found. The top mattress of the bunkbeds was missing, (One of the so-called renters took it for their kids!) so Jenna put all of Charlise's MANY stuffed animals up there. She had some white, lacy curtains that now hung in the windows, she put Charlise's porcelin dolls out, and it turned out quite nice!

A few months down the road, Nichole and her boyfriend were looking for a place to stay. She asked her Mom if they could stay in her garage, as she didn't want to disturb either of their privacy. Jenna said that was fine, but the garage was still full of stuff! Jenna had the church come and build her a ramp for the garage steps, so she was able to get in there. She had disposed of many boxes this way, cleaning dirty dishes and clothes, that had obviously been thrown in with no consequence. Nichole came over one day, to help organize the garage for their stay. Steve was there to help, also. It didn't take long, and they were butting heads!! Steve was not very understanding, Nichole got too defensive, they both blew-up, ending with Steve throwing Charlise's Huffy bike, up against the back, garage wall. It was all bent, ruined. It eventually had to be thrown out. Jenna had always remarked that if men wanted to vent their anger on "things", fine, use their own fucking stuff!! It put a rather, large hole in the garage wall, that Steve's brother came and mudded-up. He did realize, that his brother took advantage ? Their problem. Nichole never came to stay. They found an apartment in a town about 15 miles away.

In Jenna's kitchen was her china cabinet, full of her Grandmother's beautiful, antique china. Next to it, was a card table and two bent, folding chairs. Steve had kept their table and chairs from their dining room. But then, his grandma had given them to them! He could have the ugly, pieces of shit, as far as she was concerned!! The wonderful couple who had volunteered to help her, asked her one day if she would like to have their old dining set. "Absolutely! That would be so nice of you!"Jenna was thrilled! They brought her a really nice, wooden table and four chairs. It fit perfectly in the dining room, and looked good, too! Let them keep their junk, she could ALWAYS find better, somehow.

THE END OF AN ERA

Jenna had moved into her apartment in January of that year. She had had severe, menstrual problems since the last year of living in the nursing home. She was having at least two periods a month, with severe cramping, bloating, chocolate cravings, and bad PMS. Jenna went to see, yet another specialist, an OB/GYN Doctor. He took extensive ex-rays, and determined she had a few cysts, and would need a full hysterectomy. Jenna had already written and called for her Medical and accident reports, which had told her that besides her bladder, a large cyst on her remaining ovary had burst. They had also showed her a few other facts, that no one had bothered to tell her about, or maybe, were unknown even to them! So, they scheduled a hysterectomy for her. Jenna had been SO miserable with this , she was MORE than willing! She told the Doctor, "Take it all! I don't need it!" Fortunately, she was having the operation at one of her favorite hospitals, one with no students, cutting things they weren't supposed to!!

The surgery went well, with no complications. Her Dad and Step-Mom were there, which meant a lot to Jenna. After recovery, she was put in a semi-private room, with a young girl, who was scheduled for tests.Jenna was in a lot of pain! It's extra hard when you can't even re-position your booty in the bed, to find a more comfortable spot! I guess she made too many grunts of pain. Her roommate complained, and Jenna was moved to a private room. She actually did Jenna a favor! No roommate, no distractions, TV to herself, and BLESSED privacy!! After a few days of suffering, Jenna felt a little better, enough that two Aids helped Jenna take a semi-shower. She needed it! She was FUNKY!! What a difference a shower makes! She felt like a new woman. Well, maybe not a woman. Human, anyhow. For a couple of weeks after the operation, Jenna fell into the well of depression. Not only was sex a thing of the past, now her uterus had joined the many body parts of the medical dumpters! Don't get me wrong, she was glad to see the problem disappear, and knew her fertile days were long gone! She still felt "Less of a woman." Oh well, she still had the "good" parts. Cobwebs and all!! One more thing Jenna would NOT miss. Kind of like husbands! They served their purpose for a time, and then.....they went away!!

DAZED AND CONFUSED

The first summer that Jenna spent in her new "home", there were times she was dazed by happiness; fulfillment. Some days were filled with sadness; too many thoughts about what she had done, and lost. Other days were downright confusing!Some days Steve was kind, and thoughtful. On others, he was distant, and somewhat mean! Jenna grew tired of trying to figure him out. She just knew, something was up! Something other than the excuses she got from him, was causing this! She often wondered if it was even worth her questioning.

On one warm, summer day, a car pulled up, and out stepped an old friend, that Jenna hadn't seen for over 10 years! Shelly and her three brothers, lived in a foster home not far from Jenna's house. They all attended the same school. Jenna's older brother and Shelly's older brother, were the same age, and were good friends. That was how Jenna had met Shelly. After a while, Shelly's foster home broke-up, and they were all sent to a home for kids with no families. Shelly and Peter had already become close with Jenna's parents, which wasn't hard to do! As soon as they heard and told Jenna they were going to live in the home, and become wards of the state, Jenna pleaded with her parents to let them at least come for visits! We lived in a small house,so everyone knew they would not be able to live there, but, they made arrangements with the home to let them come and stay every other weekend Those were some of the best times Jenna had spent in her younger days! When Shelly came in, there were many hugs, and some tears shed, too! She said she was so grateful to all of us for taking them in. My Mom loved everybody, and everyone loved her! They spent the entire evening reminiscing, laughing, commiserating, enjoying a glass of wine, and each other's company. Jenna was sad to see her go. Jenna hopes Shelly knows how much she is missed, and greatly loved.

Another fantastic event that happened that summer, was that Charlise came for a visit! She got to stay for a whole week! This was the first time they had spent this much time together, under the same roof, since Jenna's accident. Just to hold her, smell her hair, talk honestly of their feelings,their experiences, share meals, sleep in the same room. It was pure Heaven to Jenna! It was such a relief to know she was ok! That not only was she being well taken care of, but she was happy! Like I said before, Jenna had Charlise's room all fixed up for her, and she loved it! But, once nighttime fell, Charlise came to Jenna and asked if she could sleep in her room. Jenna had set those damned porcelain dolls in her room, and she forgot that Charlise got spooked by them! Jenna's stupid hospital bed was a twin, and too small for the both to sleep comfortably. Jenna laid a comforter on top of the carpeted floor, put some pillows down, and a blanket to snuggle with. She did remember that Charlise liked to snuggle! Jenna promised Charlise that the dolls would be put away before her next visit, and there would also be night lights put into each room, so she could see her way around at night! Anything for her Girl's.

They spent a wonderful week of getting to know each other again. Every visit since has been the same. Jenna hopes that Charlise's Father and his wife, are aware of Jenna's deep gratitude for taking such good care of her. They have done a wonderful job!

In the middle of all this, Steve would still take Jenna for groceries, once a month, take her garbage to the nearest dumpster, once weekly, take her for periodic haircuts, and even out to eat occasionally!! (Yes, Jenna usually paid her own way, but he still stayed in contact!) They were still married, after all! Maybe only legally, or by name, but she could understand better, if he would just deal with it! This all made her crazy with confusion! She'd rather just have him look her in the eye, and tell her, "It's over !", if that's how he felt!! Let them both get on with their lives!! That fall, on her birthday, Steve took out for a nice dinner, where Jenna had her first real drink since her accident, because, afterwards, he took her for a tattoo! She got a fairly large dragon, on her right calf. She had heard that dragons were supposed to be a Chinese good-luck sign, and she figured she could use all the good-luck she could get! With the little bit of alcohol in her system, she was relaxed, and at peace with the whole needle thing. What was another needle? She had felt like a damn pin-cushion, for years, anyhow. Talk about confusion. Jenna didn't know if Steve was doing this out of guilt, or because he knew she had always wanted a tattoo, and was sorry she had missed getting one, because of the accident. It turned out nice, she loved it! Some of her older aids did not. SOME? All of her aids were over 50! Good thing it wasn't their stinking leg.

Jenna had FINALLY starting receiving her child support arrearage checks, from her first husband, Nichole's father. She saved them, as she knew that if Steve really wanted a divorce; she was going to hire her favorite lawyer; and make him pay.

Steve finally took her for her picture ID, and she studied all fall for her GED. They let her go ahead and register for college, and she started school, right before the tattoo. The school said that they had let her start before she even had her GED, because she had passed her entrance exams with such a high score! Jenna wanted her GED, but she also wanted college. She felt she had something to prove. Mostly, to herself. Jenna began, only taking one course, a basic computer class. She had several things to check out first. Her smarts, her stamina, other's reaction to the "chair", and how her transportation went. Luckily, the teacher was understanding, patient, and did not hesitate to help her, when she needed it. She also had a tutor/helper, from the school, with the same name as her niece, who was pleasant, and very helpful. She learned, early on, that college was a lot different than High School! It wasn't about clothes, or last names, or popularity. Intelligence, hard work, and WANTING to be there, rather than HAVING to be there, made all the difference. It was an elective, so the final grade was a satisfactory or un-satisfactory.

Jenna aced all of her tests in this course, and received an S. That December, right before Christmas, Jenna took her GED. It was at the Vocational High School, right next to the College. Nichole had attended here, her junior year, but had returned to her home school for her senior year. The test lasted two days,for about three hours each day, the most nerve-wracking part, being the Algebra! They had a typewriter they let her use for the written part, which she had no doubts of passing, as she loved to write. After the testing, she had to wait three weeks for the results. Jenna tried to stay busy during the Holiday that year, while she anxiously waited for the results.

The previous summer, her Father had told her that he had lung cancer. Ever since my Mother, and his brother had passed, he had become close with my Aunt Susie. Not on a romantic level, but, good friends, who were almost always together. Jenna was glad to see them together, so much. She knew her Mom would not have wanted her Dad to be lonely, and she thought, they both needed to stop worrying about other's so much, and have some fun!! Jenna would always be thankful to her Aunt Susie for making her Dad stop smoking. When he was diagnosed with lung cancer, his Doctor was glad that he had quit, and said they had caught it early.He right away started with cancer treatments. Radiation, and the first batch of chemo was rough going! It scared Jenna to see him with no hair, much thinner, and obviously weaker. The hardest part of all of this was her Dad had met a woman last year, and got married the previous October. He was very happy with her, and you could tell how much they loved each other, by looking at them. Some people were kind of leery of the situation, because they couldn't see or imagine him with anyone other than Mom. It had been five years since Mom had passed. It wasn't like he had picked some dame up, on the way home from the cemetery! That's another reason why passing her GED was so important to Jenna. Her family needed something up lifting, cheerful, something to celebrate. When her case worker finally called, and told her she had passed, Jenna was SO happy! She said an out loud prayer, and thanked Her Heavenly Father, for helping her with the test, looking out for her Dad and her Girl's, and keeping her sane through all of this!

Jenna ordered and bought a new artificial Christmas tree for Christmas that year. There were PARTS of two trees that Jenna had kept in her basement, at the house, but neither of them was complete. Jenna had her Aid's help her decorate that year. It looked nice, when done! After Christmas break at school, Jenna began her second semester, this time taking two classes. A more advanced Computer course, and a Basic English Composition class. To this day, she is so very thankful to have taken that Computer Class! Before, she could barely turn the thing on! It had taught her so much. It was important for schoolwork, sure, but, you almost needed computer skills just to get by on anything, anymore!!

Jenna ended up with an A in both classes that year. A 4.0 GPA. Wow. That was a new one! She had always been pretty smart, she just hadn't applied herself. Partying and getting laid had been her goals in High School!! Too bad it had taken this to convince her, that there was more to life.

UNCONDITIONAL LOVE

What a parent felt for a child, (IF they had a soul!) what a spouse was supposed to feel for their mate, and what Jenna now found with her cats. The first spring that she lived in her apartment, she had mentioned to Nichole, how much she would like to have a cat. She loved dogs as much, but knew she wouldn't be able to take care of one like she should. Jenna had lost a dog and a cat, when she lost her house. She missed them a lot. That summer, before Charlise came for her visit, Nichole brought her two kittens. A brother and sister duo. Two little balls of fluff, full of energy! Nichole gave the male his name-Nugget. And he was a little golden Nugget. Stand offish at first; very independent. When Charlise came for her visit, Jenna let her name the female. She chose the name, "Princess."That reminded Jenna of the pony her and her siblings had had, named Princess, who was anything BUT!! At the time, Jenna had a big, beautiful, Philodendron plant, in her antique, washing machine tub, in front of her front window. One of her aids had given her the start, and she had nursed it, and watched it grow into this. Jenna had always had a "Green Thumb", and loved having plants around her. Well, as the cats grew, they grew to love that plant as well! They dug in its dirt, pulled at the leaves and stems, even eating them, as outside cats will eat grass. They eventually killed it. At first, Jenna liked Princess's temperament more than Nugget's. As they grew, Princess became more trouble! She broke quite a few of Jenna's knick-knacks, and strew garbage around from the waste paper basket. Nugget grew more affectionate, more loving day by day. I had told Steve how much trouble Princess was giving me, and how I thought I might give her up. But, before I would do anything, I would make sure she at least had her shots. I made an appointment, at a local Veterinarians, and Steve took the three of us to it. I didn't have a pet carrier, so we just used collars with leashes. They were fine in the car, but, got spooked by the dogs in the waiting room. They were both good for the Vet. Nugget was a damned, good- looking cat, much prettier than his sister, but, Jenna did not appreciate what the Vet said about Princess's looks! He said, "That's an ugly cat, if I ever saw one!" I had to leave Nugget over the weekend, because of his operations; de-clawing and de-balling!! Steve told me, he knew a friend of his brother's, who was studying to be a Vet, and she would take Princess off my hands. Jenna thought that if this girl was going to be a Vet, she would give Princess a good home, and she was going with her shots. If Jenna had only known then what she knows now!! Steve was going to live with Princess too, as he was living with his brother's friend!! Another notch for the bedpost.

Nugget grew into a big cat. He weighed twenty pounds soon! But, he was very obedient, loving, and had a great personality. Even Jenna's aids grew to love him. Every morning when her morning aid came, she'd open the front door, where Nugget would be waiting. After she would tell him, "Good morning!", she would let him outside to run, and get some fresh air. He never went far, and always came back within fifteen minutes. One Sunday morning, Jenna was in the bathroom, getting dressed and ready for the day, when Nugget came to the bathroom door, meowing loudly, and acting strange! She wheeled out to the living room, where she reached down to pet him, and try and see what the matter was. Something was definitely wrong!! The more he tried to move, the stiffer he got. Within seconds, he was just dragging his rear legs. Jenna immediately began to cry. She crawled down onto the floor, and laid her head next to his. Jenna carefully stroked his fur, all the while saying,"Poor Nugget. I love you, Buddy." That was Jenna's "pet" name for him. He was her Buddy. He slept in her bed, slept on her lap, in the chair, was her constant companion, and would even give her kisses! Jenna never knew one could love a pet so much, and she had always had pets! It was trouble finding a Vet open on a Sunday, but Jenna's aid suggested the Vet not far from here. JoEllen called the emergency number, she took us there, where the Vet met us. He examined Nugget quickly, when Nugget lost control of his bowels. Jenna realized that he was dying. That he had been struck by something, and had came home to die. She looked at the Vet, tears streaming down her face, and said, "Please; put him out of his misery. I don't want him to keep suffering." He was gone in seconds. Jenna wept. The Vet asked if she would like them to take care of the body, as he knew she was unable. And, there would be no charge,even. That was the LAST thing on her mind, but later would be a comforting end to a horrible day!

Later, that evening, it was too quiet, too empty without her Nugget. Jenna cried and cried, even kept calling out his name! She really felt like she was losing it. After all she had been through, had lost, and now losing him, was just too much. Jenna cried so much, and so hard, that it started to affect her breathing. She started to hyperventilate! She called for the Ambulance. People could say she was over—acting, spazzing-out, just calling for attention, whatever they wanted.To Jenna, this was almost like losing a child. How would she cope without him?

Nugget died on a Sunday. The following Tuesday, Jenna went to school. It was hard to concentrate, but Jenna stuck it out. Her English class was last, and as she was going out the door, she stopped and talked to her Professor. Jenna fought back tears, as she explained what had happened to Nugget. She knew her teacher would understand her grief, as she raised cats, herself. When she finished telling her Professor about Nugget, her teacher asked if Jenna would be interested in having another cat. She said she had two kittens, a brother and sister, that she was looking for a home for them. Jenna was delighted at the idea! Jenna told her, "You bet! I know they would keep me busy, and keep me from missing Nugget, so much. They would have a good home." They made arrangements to bring the cats to her apartment, the very, next day. Jenna already had all of Nugget's things, so she felt ready for two new kittys. So, the next day, Ms. McCorman and a friend, brought Jenna two,new balls of fluff. Ms. McCorman raised Persian cats, and these two were part Persian and part Mutt. The male had a squished in face, like a Persian, and they were both gray and white, with long hair. Jenna fell in love, immediately! She had already named them! The male was, Jimbo, after her Father, and the female was, Willow. They made this space their territory, right away,were kind of squittish the first couple days, but quickly got used to their surroundings. Jenna had decided, before they even came home, she would never separate these two, and NEVER let them outside! Jenna loved them from the start, and visa-versa.

They were constant forms of entertainment, much better to watch than TV! One of Jenna's Aid's helped her take them to the Veterinary clinic that had taken care of Nugget. After being so kind to her, and to him, they now would receive all of her business. Poor as she was, she was more than willing to tighten her belt, and make sure they were taken care of! Jenna would have done the same with her children, (HAD) and they were like her children now. They got their shots, were de-clawed and fixed. Jenna knew how fertile cats were, and especially being siblings, she didn't need any banjo-playing kittens!! Not to mention that by time she had them de-clawed, they had already discovered that climbing the curtains was great fun! Jenna felt a bit guilty afterwards, watching them still trying to sharpen claws, that were no longer there. Nugget had done the same thing. They did make the mourning over Nugget less. Jenna had a framed picture of him in her living room, that she often looked at with admiration.

The next summer when Charlise came for her yearly visit, Jenna told her to pick which one of the cats she would like to call her own. That Mom would keep the cat here, as her Step-mom was allergic, and she had a Pit-bull at home! Charlise chose Willow. After that, Jenna talked to both cats, of Charlise, often. Her Dad and Step-Mother owned two Chihuahuas that went everywhere they went, so when they came to visit, the cats had fun chasing the dogs back and forth! Both of the dogs together didn't weigh as much as one of the cats! What an adventure!! Surprisingly, they all got along, fairly well. Jenna was so glad to have those cats. They made an empty existence, easier to endure.

EASY COME, EASY GO

Prior to losing Nugget that spring, Jenna had thrown a small party celebrating her achieving her GED. Only three couples showed up, she had invited many more. One couple was her brother and sister-in-law, one was Lee and her husband, and the other was one of her oldest friends, who had been married to Jenna's first cousin, who had succumbed to cancer, and her new fiancé. This friend, Belinda, had also been Jenna's last Matron-of-Honor, at her marriage to Steve. They all had a really good time. Jenna had ordered a cake, made some snacks, provided some beer, and made a spiked punch. A few of her guests also brought more beer and snacks. They all laughed, talked, and played some Yuker. Belinda pulled Jenna aside and tearfully told her how sorry she felt, that she knew she hadn't been a good friend lately. Jenna just told her, that no matter what had happened in the past, that she would always consider her a close friend. After they all left that night, Jenna worried about them driving home. Most of them had consumed quite a few brewski's, and Jenna knew how dangerous that ride could be!!

For several months, Jenna had been having more and worse leg spasms. Worse than before she had almost died having this Baclifen pump put in her abdomen! Doctor's visits were the worst. Having to sit and wait, the spasms would be so intense, she would have to hold tightly to the arms of her chair, so as not to be shaken out of it!! The Nero-Surgeon who had installed it, ordered ex-rays, and they found that the catheter, or tube to her spinal column was not even hooked up. They did another surgery, to fix the first surgery, botched by the students! This time, Jenna knew better than to trust them blindly, and told them beforehand, "No students allowed!!" This time, it went without a hitch. It actually performed the task it was intended to.

Jenna had been in telephone and letter writing contact with her favorite lawyer all of that summer. If Steve wanted this divorce, he could have it! But, he would pay alimony, if it killed her. Jenna had never asked for this in her previous divorces, but Steve owed it to her. He lost her house, for God's sake!! Her lawyer asked her if she had anyone who would come testify for her, about the loss of the house. Billy and Nichole both said they would provide whatever help they could be. Jenna had started a new year of college, two days before the final hearing. There had already been several meetings with a Court Mediator. These were efforts on Steve's side, to try and talk Jenna out of demanding the alimony! Well, he forgot that she had been down this road before, and after he had hurt her and her Girl's so badly, she wasn't about to give-up squat!!

Jenna had just started the new school year, and was not doing so well. She attributed it to being apprehensive about the divorce. She was even failing easy tests! Jenna just couldn't concentrate. Nichole took her to the Courthouse, the day of the trial. Billy showed up, but neither his, nor Nichole's testimony was required. Steve agreed paying less alimony than they had originally asked for, and Jenna agreed to it. Jenna knows, that by now, they both just wanted it to be OVER. What really sucked about that day, was that Steve did not even have the balls, or the class, to say Good-by to Jenna! She knew it had ended badly, that she had royally fucked-up, but so had he ! She knew how much they had once loved each other. She found it amazing, how he could turn it on and off, like a frigging faucet.

That was on a Tuesday. Jenna had school Tuesdays and Thursdays. She had taken that Tuesday off for the trial, and was too upset to go on Thursday. The following Tuesday, she went, but didn't feel very confident. The first class was English Comp. 1, a class Jenna loved, and should be able to ace! The Professor, who was an excellent teacher and was quite funny, handed back a test they had taken earlier. An F, once again. That devastated Jenna, and started her heart a-pounding! After class, she asked to be taken out for a cigarette, smoked it and tried to calm her nerves. The next class was Psychology. This was a required course, and Jenna found it very interesting. She had recently changed her major, to Social Work. Jenna had learned more about the areas of the brain, and what their functions were, than she had ever learned from the THREE Neurologists' she had!!

While sitting in the hallway, outside the Psych class, she began to feel very strange. Her heart was pounding, her breathing was difficult, and a heavy weight was crushing her chest. Just then a fellow student was walking down the hall, began to pass her, stopped, and asked if she was ok. A large majority of her fellow students were nursing students, as it was a demanded trade, these days. Jenna did not even feel like she could answer verbally, she shook her head no. The girl took off running, saying, "I'll get help! Just be a minute." Next thing Jenna knew, she was surrounded by concerned and curious by-standers. Any other time, she'd probably be embarrassed by the attention, but her chest hurt so bad, she didn't care who saw! Then, a gurney and Paramedics came rolling down the hall. They asked what was wrong, Jenna answered as best she could, they took vitals, helped her onto the gurney, and whisked her away to the waiting ambulance.Jenna's blood pressure was elevated, they did a echo-gram, and ordered more tests. She ended up being in the hospital a few days, where she had a non-stress test and was scheduled for a heart cautherization. Jenna quit smoking-AGAIN. She had the cautherization, they determined there was no blockage, that she wouldn't need a stent, and told her it had been a severe anxiety attack. It had all been just too much stress, at once! Jenna's decided it would be healthier if she took a break from school, at least for now. Between the divorce and dropping out of school,her heart was broken. Pretty much like the rest of her body.

BAD
GONE
GOOD

Jenna was to have a visit with Charlise; to actually be able to spend a Holiday with her! The first one since the accident. Jenna and Lee were still speaking at the time, and they made plans for them all to spend Fourth of July together. Charlise had seen pictures of Lee's sons before; had heard a lot about them, and was interested in meeting them. They were little Hotties! They had invited them to, and took them to, a family birthday party. The family was holding it at a shelter house, in a nearby park. The park was directly across from the High School, and that's where they were having the fireworks display. It was a very nice get-together, and Jenna and Charlise had a really good time together.

It was times like these, that sometimes really bothered Jenna, too. Like when they started playing Frisbee. Not that she didn't like the game, she just wished she could join in! This was as frustrating,as reaching for the telephone, to call her Mom, or one of her Aunts that had passed, only to remember she could not do that any longer. Even though she was finally coming to terms with her disability, it was NOT easy! She had been such an active person all her life and to just sit and watch, now, made her feel lazy.

Jenna had said thousands of prayers, asking, even begging God, :"Ok. You saved me. Now, what do You want me to do? I'll do whatever You want, I just don't know what that is yet. Please! Send me some kind of sign!" Jenna was very grateful He had helped her get her GED, and get through one year of college, she just wished she knew what to do now. She had begun school last Fall, but the final divorce hearing was two days after it started, and the stress of it all, finally did her in. She had already had a few tests, which any other time she would have aced, but she wasn't able to concentrate, and failed them. She took that year off school. Jenna had bigger Fish To Fry.

Christmas came and went, spent alone, as usual. After the Holidays, the phone rang one day, and it was Lee. She told Jenna that she had got a DWI, and rather than spend time in jail, she was to pay to spend the weekend with other offenders, and go to classes about alcohol and drugs. Jenna said how she wished they had had that when she got her DWI's, she went directly to jail! No passing GO, no $200.00 , NOTHING. Three days with the Hookers! Yeh, it sucked, alright, but, what did anyone learn? Not to get caught? Lee had told one of her "teacher's" about her, and they asked if she would like to speak. Lee informed them of her speech impediment, they asked if she was understandable, and Lee said she had no problem understanding. Lee told them what Jenna always said," If you don't understand something, just ask her to repeat it." Jenna asked Lee, "What should I say?" Just tell them what happened . How drinking and driving has changed your whole life!" Lee assured her, to just be herself. Actually, people have told Jenna since, that having the speech problem, also from the accident, lets them know, she is not acting, telling BS, she is serious! Jenna had been in the same chair these offenders now sat in. How, in the Hell, could she pass judgment? She did not want to wind-up, in this chair, that she was now in!! Same for Lee. Jenna was sorry that she got busted. She knew how stiff those fines were, what a hassle it was to find rides when your license is suspended, how much your insurance rates went up! She had been there, done that. Know how much she'd trade for that now?

Jenna's talk turned out better than she had expected it to. And, it felt SO right! She had written some things to say, on a piece of paper, beforehand. When Jenna rolled into that room, she never once, looked at the paper! She simply spoke her mind. It literally, rolled off her tongue. Almost, like someone was speaking through her. I know, that sounds- almost spooky. Well, that's how it feels.One of the worst things, that had ever been said to Jenna, was: Someone with good intentions, putting their hand on yours, and saying, "I know how you feel." How THE HELL, do you know how I feel?! Oh, you've been violently raped? Been beaten by the man whose supposed to love you so damned much? Had your "real" mother, reject you TWICE? Killed someone? Are you handicapped? Suffered the stigma's attached to having a Mental Illness? Lost your kids? Had your husband dump you, because you were now, "Damaged Goods." Oh, you don't know how I feel then.(Then get your stinking hand off me, please!) Just tell them that you're there for them. Don't get all self-righteous. They need your help, not your sermon.

Earlier, last year, Lee had hooked Jenna up to do an interview for the local paper. Lee worked there now, in the Advertising Department. Jenna ended up in the paper, with a picture of her and her first cat, Nugget, on her lap. Since that interview had gone so well, they had asked her if she would write a piece on the Life Flight Reunion , that was being held soon. A friend of Jenna's took her to this, and between the two of them, they also took a roll of pictures. Lee came to the house and picked up the story and the film. Jenna had been told, by anyone who had read it, that the story was good. She was excited to be published! It was to be her first time! The Editor used her story, alright. She put a title on it, added some, and signed her name to it. They also used Jenna's pictures! They never once mentioned that they weren't even frick'in there! Jenna threw the paper to the floor, and said a few choice words, when she read it. Next day, she called and complained to the owner. He was polite, but condescending. Eventually, Jenna just left it alone. That was pretty much the end of her and Lee's friendship. It wasn't Lee's fault her employers were crooks! And Jenna understands, when you work for someone, "Don't rock the boat!"Kiss some ass, if you have to.

Sorry things turned out this way, Lee! But, Thanks for helping me "Find My Purpose."

COMING TO TERMS

Ever since Jenna had woke-up from the coma, she had dreams or fantasies about being "cured". About walking again, about being whole.Now she was always in the wheelchair, in dreams.She had finally come to terms with being this way. Jenna realized that she could never return to being the woman she used to be. Now she was striving to be a better person. Able bodied or not! Jenna was grateful that the brain damage had not been severe enough to dismiss the things she already learned, and the ability to learn anew. Having a purpose now, gave her something to work for, look forward to. Jenna knew that if she could save ONE life with her message, she had done her job.

Jenna had been through a lot since the accident. Ten surgeries, so far. 1.) Right Femur 2.) Exploratory Surgery (on abdomen) Resulting in bladder repair and suturing ruptured ovarian cyst 3.) Surgical Openings for Colostomy and eventual Feeding Tube 4.) Tracheotomy 5.) Double Eye Repair 6.) Hemroidectomy 7.)Baclifen Pump Installation 8.)Hysterectomy 9.) Pump Repair 10.) Lumpectomy She had also had countless tests run, procedures performed, and would still like to have some cosmetic surgery! But, when you are destitute, you have to learn to live with the scars and imperfections. Jenna knows she can deal with it. She's still here, still kicking, still looking towards the future.Jenna at one time even questioned her importance in her Daughter's life. She knew that they loved her still!

Jenna wanted them to respect her , know that she was trying to take a horrible experience, and make something positive come from it.

As far as the people who had abandoned her, family, friends, or acquaintances, all she had to really say to them was, take me as I am, or SEE YA!! Jenna was done trying to be someone she thought other's wanted her to be. Just work to be THE BEST Jenna, she could be now! She had apologized for her mistakes of the past, a zillion times. That's the key word-PAST. Did they live their lives hanging their heads, never looking to the future for things they had done? What good did that do, anyhow?! It's good to be sorry. Or you are a sociopath. Just live your life doing better, never repeating it! Fame and riches were grand, sure, but all one really needed to survive was : Love, A Purpose, Determination, and Self-Respect.

Jenna wants all of those who have EVER helped her, in ANY way, to know, how very grateful she is, that she has been humbled by this entire experience, and that they should continue to reach out to those in need. Jenna will also do what she can.

To the family of the man she killed: Sorry is NOT enough. Jenna wants you to know, she would trade places with him in a SECOND, if she could! Please know, that she is trying for forgiveness by doing what she is, if there is more she needs to do, she will. His life is NOT in vain. Be healthy, happy, and do not live with hatred in your hearts. Then she will feel like she has done more damage than she already has. What she did was awful, she knows, but, she is a sincere person, who never wanted to hurt anyone.

STARTING OVER

That's exactly what Jenna was now in the process of doing. Starting over, anew, this was the NEW Jenna. The old Jenna was GONE. History. She had actually thought of having a memorial service to say good-by to her. Good-by and Good Riddance! No more drinking and drugging, whether it was to self-medicate, or bury the shame.There used to be MUCH SHAME! Shameful of bad habits, never finishing anything, like school or marriages, the shame of feeling like she was never quite up to other's standards, parenting mistakes, even her rape. Jenna being raped in 1984, had always made her feel SO dirty, like she had been to blame! She felt badly that her parents had to deal with her afterwards. They didn't know how to react, how to really help. How could they?! This had never happened to anyone they had ever known. And she couldn't help them, help her! Jenna was lost, scared, and confused herself! That's why she ran away, away from all who were close to her, afraid that her shamefulness would rub off. Jenna knows now that she should have received therapy then. More hindsight. Everyone needs therapy, at some time in their lives. We all need to talk to someone! There is NO shame in that! If you bury it, it's still there, just waiting to rear it's ugly head! The bottom line is: Problems create more problems. Fix # 1 before you deal with # 2.

Jenna heard an analogy today that was so true! About feeling like one was floating out in the ocean, surely drowning. Waiting for someone to rescue you!

Save me, PLEASE!! She was not waiting anymore. Now she was swimming! Swimming with all her might, seeing land ahead, and bound and determined to get there! And, if something did stop her, she knew she had tried. She had not quit this time! Jenna would NEVER give-up again.

There is good inside ALL people. You just have to reach down, deep inside and pull it out! She knows. Sounds easier than it is. But, you can do it!! If Jenna can, you can too. Sure, it helps to have faith in God. First, have faith in yourself! Like love, how can you truly love another, until you love yourself?! If you feel you can't love yourself, that there is nothing to love, improve your outlook, your willingness to give-up old, bad habits for new, good habits. Love will come! It's SO wonderful to wake-up now with self-confidence, about the day ahead, the future ahead! Without the help of Jenna's therapy, and now speaking to other's making the SAME mistakes she used to, she would have never have had the courage to feel confident. To Start Over.

If Jenna has hurt anyone putting her experiences, her TRUE feelings in writing, she regrets that. But, it was once said to her, "Truth Hurts."

Jenna had been legally dead. Asleep in a coma, for seven months. And, asleep to reality for most of her life. Now, she was, finally WIDE AWAKE!

About the Author

I am a small town girl, who has always had big aspirations, of being a Published Author. Anything that related to language, be it English or foreign, always created great interest, in knowing more about it. These were the subjects I fared best at, in school. I have always believed that reading is the main key to knowledge. Experience teaches many aspects we need to know, but to someone growing up with limited resources, books took us all the places, we could not go. I have never been overseas, but can tell you much concerning geography and culture. When I was a child, we did not have computers, video games, or cell phones. I was either outside enjoying the sunshine, or curled-up with a good book. I have read everything from "Little Women" to "The Exorcist." It is almost impossible to say what my favorite type literature is. I will read most anything ! I really just need a story: true, or made-up.

I am following my life-long dream in writing and publishing this account. It is an awful shame that it took this terrible incident, to bring this to fruition. I am now a permanently handicapped woman, who hopes to get two messages out to anyone willing to listen. NEVER DRINK AND DRIVE. Not only is it dangerous, it's just, plain-STUPID. There can be life after catastrophe. Yes, it has been very, very difficult. Considering what I did, I've deserved it. I have never asked to be absolved of my sin.

My goal is to provide some entertainment with this story, but to also help get a valuable lesson, to those who may need it. Please, do not think, "It will never happen to me !" Let my book and my wheelchair be proof how unlikely that is. Also remember to tell the ones you love, that you do love them. OFTEN. Things can happen when you least expect them to.

Jenna Slone